Walks in Finistère

by

Wendy Mewes

Walks in Finistère

published by Red Dog Books
ISBN 978-0-9568699-8-2

© Wendy Mewes 2016

Please note that information in this book reflects the time of writing, and that changes to footpaths and places of interest are always possible over time.

British Library Cataloguing-in-Publication Data
A catalogue record for this book is available from the British Library

All rights reserved. The publisher's prior written consent is required for any reproduction of this work, in part or in whole, in any form whatsoever.

Red Dog Books is based in Somerset and in Brittany.
Enquiries should be addressed to the editorial office at
Red Dog Books, Poullic, 29690 Berrien, France.

email: reddogbooks@orange.fr

www.reddogbooks.com

Printed and bound in China

For Tex
who thinks it was all
for his benefit anyway

WALKS IN FINISTÈRE

Introduction	page	7
Grading of walks		8
Directions		8
Map symbols		9

Town
1	**Roscoff** 6km Grade 1	11
2	**Brest** 5.75km Grade 1	14
3	**Carhaix** 4.3km Grade 1	22
4	**Quimper** 4km Grade 1	28

Country Circular Walks
5	**Menhir de Kerloas** 7.6km Grade 2	36
6	**St-Derrien** 8.1km or 13.1km Grade 2	38
7	**Lampaul-Guimiliau** 11.1km Grade 2	41
8	**Riboul Potic** 4.9km Grade 2	44
9	**Huelgoat** 12.1km Grade 2	48
10	**Gouézec** 5.5km Grade 2/3	52
11	**Locronan** 8.1km Grade 2	55
12	**Scaër** 7.5km Grade 2	59
13	**Roches du Diable** 6.5km Grade 2	62
14	**Riec-sur-Belon** 5.3km Grade 2	64
15	**Plobannalec** 6km Grade 1	66

Coast - Introduction   70

Coast Circular Walks
16	**Locquirec** 15.3km Grade 2	72
17	**Dourduff-en-Mer** 7.5km Grade 2	76
18	**St-Michel** 5km Grade 1	79
19	**Trémazan** 12km Grade 1	82
20	**Pointe de Doubidy** 9km Grade 2	85
21	**Menez Dregan** 7.2km Grade 1	88
22	**Penmarc'h** 12.4km Grade 1	92
23	**Doëlan** 5.2km Grade 1	96

Coast Linear Walks

24	**Meneham** Grade 1	98
25	**Le Conquet to Fort de Berthaume**	
	12.5km Grade 2	100
26	**Landévennec** 8km Grade 2	104
27	**Château de Dinan to Cap de la Chèvre**	
	9.9km Grade 3	107
28	**Pointe du Millier to Kastel Koz**	
	9.6km Grade 3	110

Feature - The Monts d'Arrée 114

Walk 1 **Lac St-Michel and the Yeun Elez**
circular Grade 1 15km 118
Walk 2 **La Feuillée** circular Grade 2 8.2km 120
Walk 3 **Along the Crests** linear Grade 2 15km 121
Walk 4 **Mougau** circular Grade 3 13km 122

Feature - Nantes-Brest Canal 126

Walk 1 **Pont de Goariva - Pont Daoulas**
linear Grade 1 3.7km 128
Walk 2 **Gwaker - Châteauneuf-du-Faou**
linear Grade 1 7km 130
Walk 3 **Keriégu - Ty Men** linear Grade 1 5.3km 133
Walk 4 **Pont Coblant** circular Grade 2 8.4km 135

Feature - Ouessant 138

Walk 1 **Le Stiff to Lampaul** via the north coast
linear Grade 1 10.4km 142
Walk 2 **Lampaul to Pointe de Pern**
circular Grade 1 8.25km 143
Walk 3 **Le Stiff to Lampaul** via the south coast
linear Grade 1 16.8km 144

Index 148
Glossary 150

INTRODUCTION

Finistère has so much variety of landscape and paths to offer walkers of all types, that I'm pleased to present this second collection of walks in the far west of Brittany. The chosen routes once again cover coast, country and town, with a range of distances and levels of effort, but without any intention of achieving a neat and even spread over the department - some areas are much more interesting than others in terms of landscape.

New this time are features on particularly rich areas for walkers: the Monts d'Arrée, the Nantes-Brest Canal and the island of Ouessant. These multi-page sections give an overview of the possibilities, full maps and some specific recommendations, my idea being that some people will like to spend a few days or a weekend exploring the same location. I have also included linear suggestions for coastal and canal locations in this volume, where these provide better interest than an artificial 'circuit' involving lots of road walking. This selection is intended to direct walkers to exceptionally attractive parts of a much greater whole. These additions to a conventional book of circular walks have been requested by earlier readers.

Many of the walks are strong on historical interest, with reference to structures like the Neolithic monuments, economic exploitation of the land and sites of significant events. Others are simply routes where nature can be enjoyed at short or long range and the sheer pleasure of being outdoors in such surroundings is reward enough for the effort involved. Where space permits, I have tried to give an idea of interesting visits in the vicinity of the walks, many of which are envisaged as half-day, leaving time for another way of getting to know the region. Where appropriate, add-ons for extending walks are suggested for those who prefer a longer trek.

The text has not been over-laden with directions, as much work has been done to ensure the maps are clear and comprehensive. Specific advice is given only where the situation is confusing or complicated on the ground. Descriptions of things to see along the way are included and other information of relevant interest to enhance the walks.

I hope there is something here for every walker to enjoy, regardless of age or ability.

Happy walking!

Wendy Mewes

GRADING OF WALKS

None of the walks in this book should pose any problem for confident and experienced walkers, although special care is needed by all on coastal routes (see below).
Grade 1 Easy, with mostly flat routes and straightforward paths.
Grade 2 Moderate, with routes which can include steady inclines, some steps and (seasonally) boggy paths.
Grade 3 Rougher terrain, and routes may include steep and/or prolonged ascents and descents (with or without steps), rocky paths and scrambles.

DIRECTIONS

In this book I have given far less emphasis than in earlier works to written directions, as the mapping has been developed to provide clarity of route marking. The walks are therefore designed to be followed from the maps, which give clear orientation at each junction of the path with arrows showing the direction to take. Where there is complication on the ground, indications are given in words in the Directions box, and this also contains details of alternatives if relevant - for example, a straightforward road route is sometimes offered instead of a challenging path to give walkers a choice if time or energy is limited. This method of presenting the walks in an accurate and easy to follow way has been successfully tried and tested.

ADVICE TO WALKERS

If walking alone, it is always a good idea to let someone know your start/finish point and approximate timings. Carrying a mobile phone and a whistle are also sensible precautions in case of emergency. The Europe-wide number to phone for help is 112, or call 15 for SAMU (French medical aid). Particular care should be taken on the coastal walks where sudden, strong winds are not uncommon, there is little shelter from sun or storm, and cliff-paths are often narrow and with unstable surfaces. On many of the routes in this book there are no direct refreshment options, so carrying water is always advised at any time of year, but please remember that a small bottle will not be sufficient on hot summer days. These basic measures of common sense are self-evident but always worth repeating. It is also advisable to wear purpose-made walking-footwear - no guarantee of dry or smooth paths offered!

KEY TO MAP SYMBOLS

- any tarmac surfaced road*
- track - anything from a carriage-width grassy path to a muddy farm track or a hard stony road
- footpath - any walkable route that isn't a track or a road
- causeway
- route to walk
- alternative route, extension or short-cut
- cycle path
- go up steps
- go down steps
- P parking
- abbey
- church in *bourg*
- chapel
- cross/*calvaire*
- cemetery
- *fontaine* (spring)
- *lavoir* (washing place)
- water tower
- sports ground
- park or garden
- town walls
- approximate extent of hamlet
- farm/farm building(s)
- house or small building
- TO tourist office
- camp-site
- picnic area
- light-house
- viewpoint
- rocks/crags
- peak
- peat bog
- monument/memorial
- cascade
- water mill
- other remarkable feature
- *menhir* (standing stone)
- *dolmen* (Neolithic burial chamber)
- museum

N.B. Each map has its own scale.

Map Symbols   *page 9*

No.1 ROSCOFF — Circular — Grade 1 — 6km

Roscoff's history of prosperity from maritime commerce, piracy and smuggling has left the town a rich architectural legacy. Wealthy ship owners (*armateurs*) traded with Spain and Portugal, Flemish and Baltic towns, carrying cargoes of wine, grain and Breton cloth. Many Roscovite captains became corsairs, licensed to attack enemy ships and confiscate their goods, when France was at war with England.

In the 18th century, when English import duties were sky-high, the smuggling of tea, wine and spirits became another lucrative outlet. During the 19th century, vegetables grown in the Léon region became important exports, most famously the *oignons rose* of Roscoff. Other developments in the town included thalassotherapy, a famous biological research centre and the study of Brittany's many seaweeds. The ferry port at nearby Bloscon was created in the 1970s, when Brittany Ferries began its regular sailings to Plymouth. This walk takes in the main sights, and could be combined with a trip to the Île de Batz (10 minute boat ride) or the *Jardin exotique* near the ferry port.

Starting point: park anywhere in the old port and walk to the far end, Quai Parmentier.

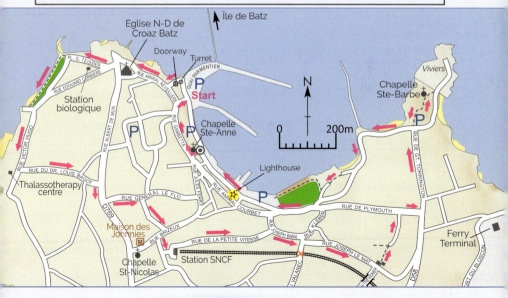

Roscoff — page 11

From the port parking, *pass remains of the old ramparts, including a corner turret shaped like a pepper-pot.*

On the left is a blocked ornate doorway, all that is left of a chapel said to have been endowed by Mary Stuart. Mary, queen of Scotland since she was just six days old, landed here in 1548 at the age of 6, on her way to Paris and future marriage with the Dauphin of France.

Follow the rue Amiral Reveillère *with its impressive houses to a large square by the church.*

On the north side, ornate cellar-entrances reflecting the wealth of Roscoff merchants can be seen, and a house with elaborate carvings, including an onion seller and a creature playing the Breton *bombarde*.

Cellar entrances

Église Notre-Dame de Croaz Batz, in Flamboyant Gothic style, was built between 1522 and 1545, financed by rich ship-owners who benefited from *corsaire* activity. The ships carved on the exterior are a reminder of this. The bell-tower was a later addition (1585) in the new Renaissance style. High up, two stone cannon point towards England.

There are two ossuaries within the church precinct, and a funerary monument to Dorothy Silburne, a London society lady who passed the last years of her life here, helping the poor. Inside the church two further British connections can be found: the magnificent 15th century alabaster altarpiece made in Nottingham, and the organ, originally made by Thomas Harrison.

Ship carved on church

Take Place Georges Teissier *along past the Station biologique.*

Station biologique This renowned scientific research centre opened in 1872 under the auspices of Henri de Lacaze-Duthiers. He was determined to establish zoology as a truly experimental science, carefully choosing this remarkable natural setting for his foundation. After WWII Georges Teissier expanded the facilities to include the new discipline of oceanography.

On reaching the coast, continue left, along rue Victor Hugo to the main thalassotherapy establishment.

Turn inland along the rue Docteur Bagot, turn right on the main road and then go first left (Rue Général Le Flo).

Take the first right, and at the end of this road turn right then left to the station to continue the walk, or detour right to the Maison des Johnnies near the Chapelle St-Nicolas in rue Brizeux.

Maison des Johnnies contains a wealth of artefacts and visual evidence telling the extraordinary story of the Breton Johnnies who, from 1828 onwards, crossed the Channel with their bicycles to sell local onions - the famous *oignon rose* - in the UK.

Continue left of the station building, straight ahead through the parking, then along rue Joseph Bara, then rue Joseph Le Mat, to a narrow grassy footpath on the left by a low stone wall. Follow this to join Rue de Plymouth (see map). Take rue de Great Torrington (town in Devon twinned with Roscoff) to the Chapelle Ste-Barbe on its lofty pinnacle.

This chapel was built in 1619, for its patron Saint Barbara (originally a Dutch cult brought back to Brittany by sailors) often invoked in times of sudden danger and threat of accidental death. It was a natural focus for those risking their lives at sea, and the white-washed chapel itself provided a helpful daymark for shipping. Johnnies leaving harbour lowered and hoisted their sails to honour the saint. There are fine views from this prominent point.

Chapelle Ste-Barbe

To complete the circuit, follow the coast once more and return through the old port, past the lighthouse (1934), which is visitable in summer, and the little Chapelle Ste-Anne (1640) now used for exhibitions. The rue Gambetta is an attractive street of old houses which leads back to the starting point at the port.

No.2 BREST — Circular — Grade 2 — 5.75km

Brest is sometimes disregarded for its superficially monotonous post-war reconstruction, but in fact there is historical, architectural and artistic interest at almost every turn, with many unusual sights. This walk takes in the best of old and new on both sides of the Penfeld river.

The site at the mouth of the Penfeld has remarkable natural advantages in the large sheltered harbour facilities of the Rade de Brest, separated from the Atlantic by a narrow channel, the Goulet. Fortified at least since Roman times, Brest was taken by the English during the 14th century Wars of Succession and only returned to the Duke of Brittany by Richard II in 1397. It was Cardinal Richelieu who determined to develop the potential of the port, ordering an arsenal to be built on the banks of the Penfeld in 1631. Here ships were constructed and fitted out, with all the relevant trades and resources assembled on one site. Since that time it has remained the most important French Atlantic naval base.

During the Anglo-Dutch threat of the late 17th century, Louis XIV's chief engineer Vauban was responsible for improving the defences of the town, his strategic plan correlating the fire-power of guns on both sides of the Goulet. The arsenal was greatly developed during the mid 18th century by Antoine Choquet de Lindu, a local marine engineer, who also built the *bagne* (prison) which provided forced labour in the shipyards. This dominated the left bank of the Penfeld until its destruction after WWII.

During the war, Brest was a major strategic site for the occupying German forces as a submarine base for operations in the Atlantic. The huge structure for housing the pens was built in 1941-2, its thick concrete resisting intense bombing raids until damage was inflicted by the new Tallboy bombs in August 1944. Much of the city was destroyed in these campaigns, hence the predominantly post-war style of architecture, when re-building had to be swift to re-house the population. The extraordinary underground shelter, L'Abri Sadi Carnot, can be visited for a vivid sense of conditions at this tragic period of the city's history. Some pockets of the old city remain and can be seen on this walk.

Starting point: The route starts from the large parking area below the ramparts, just behind the commercial port. From here, a series of stone staircases leads up to the Cours Dajot.

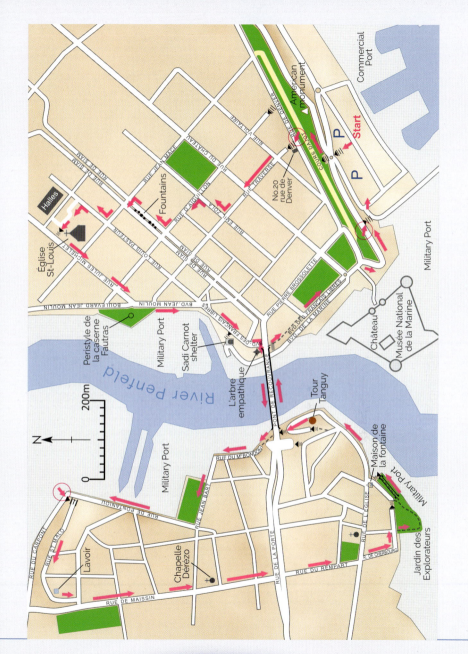

Brest

Go up the steps from the car-park, cross two roads to other side of the roundabout and take steps up to the Cours Dajot.

Cours Dajot This 600m promenade was constructed by prisoners from the nearby *bagne* (naval prison) in 1769. It provides panoramic views over the port and the Rade de Brest, a roadstead linked to the Atlantic by the narrow channel of the Goulet.

Cours Dajot

Turn right towards the American monument.

American monument The striking granite tower protruding from the ramparts is a 50m monument to American naval forces of WWI. First built in the early 1930s, it was destroyed by the Germans during WWII (because used with the lighthouse at Portzic as a sightline by RAF bombers) and then reconstructed exactly in 1958. A plaque in the little park beside it honours the Comte de Rochambeau and the Comte de Grasse, two French heroes of the American War of Independence, who sailed from Brest in 1780/1.

Cross the Cours Dajot and rue de Denver to go up steps to rue Traverse and continue ahead.

No.20 rue de Denver Beside the steps leading to rue Traverse is an *art nouveau* building (1900) by architect Sylvain Crosnier, using brick motif on the upper floor and an array of balconied windows.

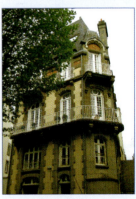

Art nouveau

Continue past art gallery on left, turn right up rue Émile Zola, then left on rue d'Aiguillon.

Musée des Beaux Arts The city's art gallery contains changing exhibitions and a fine permanent collection including many Breton subjects and examples of the Pont Aven school. It also has a pioneering art-lending facility.

No.27 Rue d'Aiguillon This house (1926) by architect Aimé Freyssinet has an exceptional display of bay windows arranged with Art deco chic.

 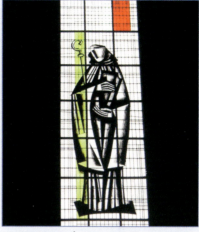

Rue de Siam   *Église St-Louis*

Turn right along rue de Siam, then left at rue Jean Mace and first right to reach the church, Église St-Louis.

Rue de Siam This is the main shopping street of Brest, linking the Place de la Liberté and the Town Hall (1961) with the Pont de Recouvrance over the Penfeld. It gets its name from a visit of ambassadors from the King of Siam in 1686 on their way to see Louis XIV at Versailles. Here it is apparent that the architecture of post-war Brest is both emblematic of 1950s style and yet retains an echo of past neo-classicism.

Place des lacs A controversial street sculpture (1986) by artist Marta Pan, originally intended as part of a much larger sequence of installations leading down to the Penfeld river, was to highlight the city's connection with sea. Called The Fountains by locals, it is made of black granite from South Africa and pink granite from Brittany.

Église St-Louis This luminous building of remarkable volume, consecrated in 1958, was a new version of the church here almost completely destroyed during the war. The exterior shows a contrasting use of concrete and the warm ochre tones of Logonna stone. Inside, the same artistic motif can be seen in the vast, almost blank, Wall of Lamentation contrasting with a flood of light through modern stained glass windows (presenting stylised figures of Breton saints) opposite.

Go round to back of church (Halles on right) and down steps into rue Michelet, turn left downhill.

At the bottom *(peristyle de la Caserne Fautras in a little garden opposite) bear left through garden. Views over Penfeld and bridge ahead, looking down on dry dock.*

Peristyle de la Caserne Fautras This 19th century arch, remnant of a pavilion from the barracks which housed naval forces from 1730, was remounted in its garden setting in 1963.

Optional - *go down steps to Sadi Carnot shelter in rampart wall, then return.*

Sadi Carnot shelter The public entrance to this vast (400m) WWII shelter can be found below (steps) in the Boulevard de la Marine near the Porte Tourville. It extends under the city as far as the Place Sadi Carnot. Built for civilians in 1942-3 as an air-raid shelter, the tunnel was also used by Germans (port end) in 1944. A detailed exhibition inside records the terrible experiences of a city at war, including a fire in the tunnel which trapped and killed hundreds.

Sadi Carnot shelter

Penfeld The original settlement of Brest was around this river. From the 17th century it was extensively developed to accommodate the needs of the French naval base, with the Arsenal providing mass employment for fitting out ships in a huge ensemble of quays, dry-docks, shipyards and industrial units.

River Penfeld, Tour Tanguy and the Pont de Recouvrance

Continue towards bridge, *past tree sculpture, and cross the river.*

L'arbre empathique This tree sculpture by Enric Ruiz Geli presents a harmony between two worlds, being both metallic and natural, with real foliage sprouting from the branches in season.

Pont de Recouvrance Opened in 1954 and replacing an earlier turning version, this bridge links the rue de Siam and the quarter of Recouvrance on the right bank of the Penfeld river. It has been modified in recent years (2011) to accommodate the new tramway system.

Turn immediately right *over the bridge, past two bollards. Go ahead through a parking area (rue du Maitre Bondon), follow round through Place Jean Bart (with a park on the right) and turn right along rue de Pontaniou.*

Recouvrance This distinctive part of the city housed sailors and workers employed in the arsenal and naval yards. It also preserves some glimpses of an earlier world than the modern city offers.

Continue straight ahead *to a 90° left hand bend where there are flights of steps leading down into the rue St-Malo.*

Rue St-Malo This is one of the few surviving old streets of Brest, retaining its character in the small terraced houses, some un-renovated, art-work and flowery decorations. An association, Vivre La Rue, works to preserve the street and encourage artistic activity here. At the top of the street is a huge double *lavoir* and drying area enclosed by walls.

Rue St-Malo

Go up rue St-Malo, *all the way up the hill and come up to main road, rue de Maissin. Turn left and follow it down (past Chapelle Dérézo) to rue de la Porte.*

Chapelle Dérézo This chapel on the site of an older church destroyed in WWII was inaugurated in 1952 in a familiar reconstruction style of granite and concrete under the name Bonne Nouvelle de Kervéguen. Deconsecrated, it has housed the theatre company Dérézo since 2011.

Cross over rue de la Porte and go up rue du Rempart to the top, with a square and a church to the left. Cross road ahead, bearing left, and turn right down rue de Cherbourg. Follow it 90° left and enter park on right. Continue round park to the left and then over walkway above gardens.

Château viewed from the Jardin des Explorateurs

Jardin des Explorateurs The garden illustrates the plants brought back from around the world by maritime explorers. It has been created on the site of a former artillery battery, and offers great views over the Rade (and, across the water, the Presqu'ile de Plougastel), the château and the mouth of the Penfeld.

Down steps and cross the road to see Maison de la Fontaine.

Maison de la Fontaine (18, rue de l'Église) This house dates from the 18th century and represents a type common in the city before the ravages of WWII. It was the property of the marine sculptor Yves Collet from 1825. The classically symmetrical façade has a monumental doorway with Ionic pilasters. The building contrasts the light stone of Logonna with darker Kersanton. A fountain was constructed on the gable end in 1791, and the medieval cross is a legacy of a nearby cemetery for victims of drowning.

Then go right downhill steeply, following wall (rue de l'église), past entrance to military port, and reach the Tour Tanguy.

Tour Tanguy Originally part of the medieval city's defences, the tower was turned into a house in the 19th century, badly damaged in WWII and then completely restored in 1964. It contains an excellent museum of Brest's history, well worth a visit.

Return over the bridge and turn right towards the château.

The Château and Marine Museum The impressive château was restored after WWII damage and today houses a well-displayed maritime museum which gives the flavour of Brest's international connections. A visit offers access to the external defensive works and unforgettable views over the Penfeld and the Rade de Brest. On the way to the entrance, there's an extensive section of tiled layers from the wall of a 3rd century Roman castellum, which took over this fortified spot of the Osismes tribe. In the medieval period it was in the hands of the Counts of Léon, until sold by one in need of money to the Duke of Brittany. The 13th century Tour Azénor is named after a legendary princess who was imprisoned here in 537 after false accusations of infidelity by her step-mother. In the late 17th century the château was greatly marked by Vauban who installed gun-emplacements and reinforced the defensive walls between the towers. The headquarters of the French navy's Atlantic Command is contained within the château's precinct.

Past the château, either cross and take Cours Dajot and back down steps or follow road round and back down steps into parking area.

Roman wall

No.3 CARHAIX   Circular   Grade 1   4.3km

Carhaix (or Vorgium) was built in the Roman era on a plateau above the valley of the Hyères in the territory of the Osismes Celtic tribe. Archaeological investigation shows that it had the typical attributes of a grid-plan of streets, where shops and houses have been excavated, as well as traces of an elaborate aqueduct system. A major new visitor site and state-of-the-art interpretation centre on this theme is due to open in rue Doctor Menguy in 2016.

Whilst it is not the most physically attractive of towns, Carhaix offers a wealth of interesting historical detail to the discerning, covering more than 2000 years of social, economic and architectural development. It was an important centre of the peasant uprising of the Bonnets rouges in 1675, a protest instigated by newly imposed taxes on stamped paper needed for all legal transactions, but broadening into a crusade against aristocratic abuses of power. From its role as head of the medieval district of the Poher to its former status as a major railway junction to the modern commercial range which includes Breton beer-making and a milk factory built with Chinese investment, Carhaix also presents an intriguing example of adaptability and enterprise. It is a forceful centre of Breton culture. A sound installation in the place du Champ de Foire honours the Goadec sisters, famous exponents of the traditional *kan ha diskan* form of call and counter-call where singers lead the moves of Breton dance.

The name is of uncertain derivation. If Kaer/Caer = a fortified place, some like to see an additional reference to the legendary Breton princess or sea goddess Ahès, but others more prosaically link Carhaix with Carofes, a crossroads, which has always been a crucial facet of the settlement, as a hub of communication radiating in all directions. It merged with nearby Plouguer in 1957 to become Carhaix-Plouguer.

Starting point: Carhaix is at the mid point of the eastern border of Finistère, just north of the central east/west route N164.
The walk starts at the **Église de St-Trémeur** (see map).

Cross straight ahead at the mini-roundabout, along rue de l'Église and bear right at junction to reach the **Église St-Pierre**.

Église de St-Trémeur The legend of Trémeur is important in the Breton oral tradition. This young boy was the son of the harsh ruler Conomor, an historical figure of the 6th century whose personage has also entered the legendary world as the Breton Bluebeard. Because of a prophecy that his son would kill and succeed him, he made attack the best part of defence, searched out and decapitated Trémeur, whose mother Tréphine had escaped her violent husband and hidden the boy for years. The statue on the west face of the church shows the child holding his own severed head. Conomor was eventually killed in battle by his step-son Judual.

St Trémeur, holding his severed head

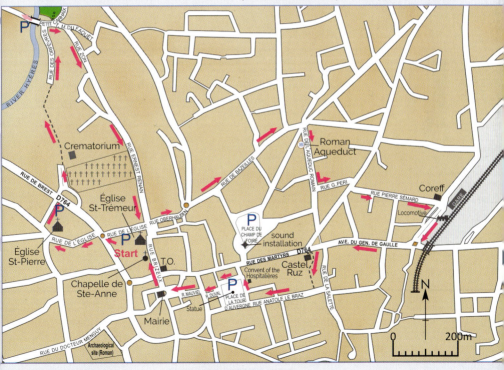

Carhaix — page 23

Église St-Pierre This church - originally the parish church of Plouguer - dates from the second half of the 11th century and Romanesque arches remain in the transept. It was restored in the 16th century and the tower constructed then. About two hundred years later the porch and choir were renewed.

Cross the parking area in front of the church to the main road, cross and take the little road down towards the crematorium. Continue downhill past this on a footpath. At the end, continue on the road down to the bridge over the Hyères.

View from across the bridge over the river Hyères

This was once the main route to Morlaix, with a toll to pay on passage over the bridge for carts and traders. The area is known as **Petit Carhaix**, formerly a sector of artisans and industrial activity such as preparation of skins for the tanning process. There were also once paper and flour mills on the Hyères. There is a little park beside the river here, and across the bridge many examples of typical old cottages and the view in the photo above.

*Go uphill bearing right on rue Zon which becomes rue Ernest Renan, back up to the town. Turn left and continue ahead for 550m, passing the site of remains of old houses. At a major junction take the second right, rue de l'Aqueduc romain, where a small section of the **Roman aqueduct** can be seen.*

Water was brought to the new town from 27km away near Paule. This triumph of engineering was a typical example of the benefits of Roman civilization. It delivered 6000m³ of water each day. To cross the valley of Kerampest to the east of Carhaix a bridge (13m high, 900m long) was built, although nothing remains of that today. Water arrived at a tower near the end of the bridge, and lead pipes took the supply all over the town. The conduit was about 0.6m wide and 0.9m high, made of stone and lined with concrete (lime, sand and ground slate).

Turn left along rue Gabriel Peri, *then right and immediately left (rue Pierre Sémard) down towards the station.*

On the corner are the premises of **Coreff**, a brewery (*brasserie*) producing excellent Breton beer. It was the first of the micro-breweries - founded in Morlaix in 1985, with British advice - which are now so successful in Brittany. The name means barley beer. There is a shop, and guided tours are arranged at certain times. It also has an exhibition space with the history of the brewery and aspects of Breton culture, the two things being closely connected!

Roman aqueduct

La Gare In 1888, a station was built at Carhaix to become the hub of a metre-gauge network in western Brittany, the *Reseau breton*. Here, five lines converged: north to Morlaix, north-east to Paimpol via Guingamp, east to La Brohinière (not far from Rennes), south to Rosporden and west to Camaret at the end of the Crozon peninsula. This provided up to 500 jobs in Carhaix with all the associated trades of the station-yard, and was crucial to the vitality and commerce of the town and its thriving markets. Today only the Carhaix-Guingamp route remains open.

Turn right and cross the road *to see an example of an engine used on the Réseau Breton.*

La Locomotive At the time of writing this railway engine (Series E410-E417) sits rather forlornly beside the road near the station, but it is in need of renovation and may be removed for that purpose. This steam engine built for the metric gauge could pull 270 tons. When the lines closed in 1967, the *Réseau breton* engines were dispersed all over France and Switzerland. This is the only one remaining in Brittany.

Piguet Mallet No. E415

Go straight on *to the main road and turn right. Continue ahead for 350m to an imposing château on the left.*

Castel Ruz (Château rouge) This dates from the early 20th century, a contemporary of the Château de Trévarez which is also in red brick. It was built for Constant Lancien, a local lawyer, with a park and stables adjoining. During WWII it was occupied by the Germans and prisoners were tortured in the basement. Purchased by the town in 1956, it has since been a tax office, then a library and music school.

Go through to the park behind the château *(use rue de la Salette if no access) where there are various examples of medieval stonework and a dovecote. Continue through the back gate and turn right along rue Anatole Le Braz. This leads to the Place de la Tour d'Auvergne and a statue of the great man himself.*

Castel Ruz

Théophile-Malo Corret de la Tour d'Auvergne
La Tour d'Auvergne (1743-1800) was an illustrious soldier and scholar, born in Carhaix. He was the great-grandson of the illegitimate son of Henri de la Tour d'Auvergne, duc de Bouillon. He was a lieutenant, then captain in the French army during war against England, soon known for his outstanding courage. He was instrumental in taking Saint-Sébastien in 1791. He refused all honours and insisted on remaining a common soldier despite his remarkable military record which continued after the Revolution, and despite Napoléon naming him *Premier grenadier de la Republique*. He died at the Battle of Oberhausen in 1800 having signed up - after retirement - in place of the only son of a close friend.

Statue in Place de la Tour d'Auvergne

A noted 'Celtomane' and historical researcher, La Tour d'Auvergne was also a gifted linguist and Breton speaker. He invented the terms *dolmen* (stone table) for Neolithic burial chambers and *menhir* (long stone) for Neolithic standing-stones (see p.68). He published his *Origines gauloise* in 1797 on release from a prison ship in England.

On the eastern side of the square are the remains of the Convent of the Hospitalières, who originally cared for the poor and sick in rue Brizeux (see below) before this building was erected in 1698. The nuns were evicted at the time of the Revolution and the convent used as a prison during the Terror. Today it is private property.

Go across the square and follow rue Duval and rue Mauviel to the Place de la Mairie.

Place de la Marie This once contained the market-hall before it was destroyed at the end of the 19th century and a new one built near the church of St-Trémeur. The attractive 17th century house with an ornate doorway on the right used to house the Commission des Eaux et Forêts (Water and Forests). It is now offices of the Poher newspaper.

Turn right along rue Brizeux (old houses) and then cross the main road to continue ahead, still the rue Brizeux.

On the corner, at the original crossroads of the town centre, is the **Maison du Sénéchal**, an impressive house of granite and slate built in the second half of the 16th century and restored in 1606 after the violence of the Wars of Religion. The *sénéchal* was an important judicial official of the king, so the rich decoration of this house suggests it may have belonged to someone of such status. Carved figures on the façade represent all levels of society: a peasant, tanner, nobleman, soldier and priest. The building now houses the tourist office. Many fine features are retained in the interior.

In rue Brizeux is the **Chapelle de Ste-Anne**, a 19th century Neo-gothic re-building of an earlier structure (1478) which was the first hospital in the town, founded by a nobleman to atone for his sins in war.

Turn left to return to the parking by the church and the starting point.

Maison du Sénéchal

No.4 QUIMPER Circular Grade 2 4km

Quimper, the small but beautiful departmental capital, is built around the river Odet with its many flowery *passerelles* and below the green hump of Mt Frugy.

The first settlement in the Gallo-Romano period was downstream at Locmaria, still the pottery centre today as then. According to legend, King Gradlon founded Quimper upstream on the opposite bank in the 5th century. Today it retains much exceptional architecture, including remains of the original fortifications and medieval houses, cultural interest of all kinds, shops and restaurants for every taste and alluring green spaces.

In an unusual historical development, the central area within the former town walls (*ville close*) was the province of the bishop and subject to religious rule, whilst the duke had to content himself with secular authority beyond the river Steir, a situation echoed in the square called place Terre au Duc. A very small château squeezed into the corner of the old town did not last long. The Franciscan convent which dominated that area was destroyed in the 19th century for the building of the covered market, today a delight for food shopping and refreshments. A staunchly bourgeois bastion in the late 19th/20th century, Quimper was proud of its self-liberation in WWII, although a high toll was paid by the Resistance fighters. One risked his life to hang the French flag from the cathedral spire when the ordeal of occupation seemed over; many were to die when the Germans returned with reinforcements.

This walk takes in the main sights and some small details of the main town and the quarter of Locmaria, which is just as remarkable in its own way and merits exploration.

Starting point: The walk starts from the Cathedral of St-Corentin (see map).

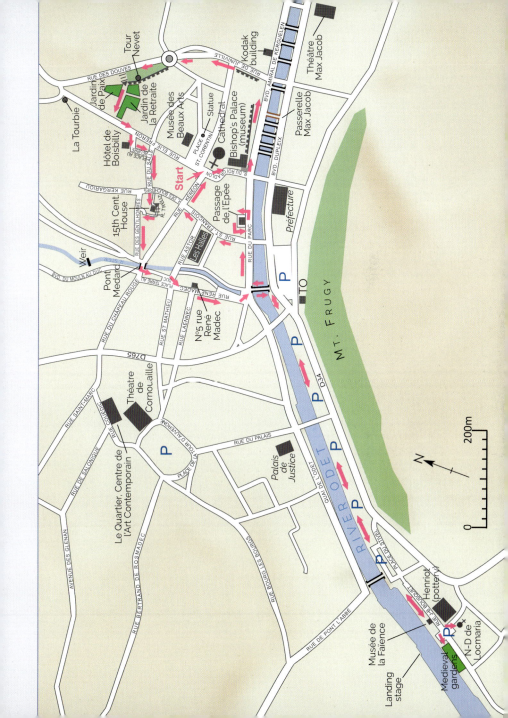

Cathedral of St-Corentin An equestrian statue of King Gradlon, legendary founder of Quimper, sits between the spires of this magnificent Gothic cathedral. When out hunting, he discovered the hermit Corentin, who lived on a single regenerating fish, and persuaded him to be the first bishop of the new city. The story is told in stained glass in the chapel of St-Corentin inside. An historical figure of equal local significance is Santig Du, the little black saint, a Franciscan who tended the sick here in the 14th century. His statue and the relic of his skull are displayed at the end of the southern aisle. Invoked for finding lost objects, grateful recipients of his help offer loaves of bread for the poor on the table provided, a tradition dating back hundreds of years and still going strong.

The cathedral was begun in the 13th century; a second building phase in the 15th saw the addition of the nave at a crooked angle. Various reasons are put forward to explain this notable trait: the proximity of the river, the line of an earlier chapel and the positioning of the (now adjoining) bishop's palace in the interim. The extra half-chapel inside on the south aisle compensates for the angle. The spires were a mid-19th century addition to the towers, previously capped with metal cones. Shops and inns were once built right along the exterior wall of the cathedral, often providing a noisy background to services inside. At the Revolution, statues were taken out of the church and burnt in the square.

Cathedral

The Place St-Corentin, which has a skating rink at Christmas, contains the **Musée des Beaux Arts**, well worth a visit if only for the paintings of Breton scenes, and a **statue of René Laennec** (1781-1826), who was born in Quimper and later practised medicine in Paris. He was the inventor of the stethoscope, and ironically died of tuberculosis after being diagnosed with that instrument by his nephew.

Go back past the main cathedral entrance.

The Bishop's Palace next door houses an exceptional museum, the **Musée Départemental Breton**, with a selection of exquisite local artefacts from each period of history, and is an interesting building in itself. You can go into the foyer to see the old kitchen (1645) with its well, ovens and service doors without entering the museum. The central tower (Tour de Rohan) remains from an earlier structure and has a wide turning stone stair and parasol roof in oak at the top. **www.museedepartementalbreton.fr**

Place St-Corentin

Continue through the Bishop's Garden if the gate is open, or by rue Roi Gradlon to the river with its passerelles. These are the legacy of grand houses on the opposite bank each with individual access to the centre.

Turn left and keep next to the water as far as the distinctive wrought-iron bridge, **Passerelle Max Jacob**.

This was erected in 1994 to commemorate the 50th anniversary of the Quimper-born artist writer and visionary (b.1876), who died in the camp of Drancy in 1944. Jacob had converted from Judaism to Catholicism at the age of 40, with his close friend Picasso standing as sponsor, but was nevertheless interred by the Germans despite international protests. He had spent much of his adult life in the Bohemian demi-monde of Paris. A copy of Modigliani's portrait of Jacob can be seen on the support under the bridge if the water is low enough. The town art gallery has a room devoted to the work of Max Jacob and his circle. In one of history's ironic twists, the Ouest-France building across the river, in 'steamboat' style, was the design of Olier Mordrel, architect, Breton nationalist and German collaborator, who worked in Quimper in the 1920s. He also designed the Kodak building further along this street.

Turn left (rue de Juniville) and continue ahead past sections of old walls to a roundabout. Here continue up rue des Douves.

The only remaining defensive tower of the medieval walled city, the **Tour de Névet**, dates from the 13th century, and was adapted for artillery in the 14th as the lower openings show. The pepper-pot roof was added later when it became a dwelling.

Go up the steps just past the tower and into the gardens.

Up steps immediately to the right is the newly established **Jardin de Paix** (Peace Garden), set out in Mediterranean style, with a terrace overlooking the town. Below is the attractive refuge of the **Jardin de la Retraite**, with its three spaces: a palm garden with fountain, a 'dry' garden with a wonderful chestnut tree and the tropical garden with banana plants, all set within ancient walls. It was once the canons' garden and also a cemetery.

Jardin de la Retraite

Go through the garden and turn left down rue Elie Fréron and almost immediately right along rue ar Barzh Kadiou.

Note the plaque on the wall which explains the name. A bard named Cadiou was hired by Hoël, Duke of Cornouaille, in 1069, according to a document from the abbey at Quimperlé.

The **Hôtel de Boisbilly**, named for an illustrious canon of the cathedral who once lived here, is a fine example of 17th century refined taste, with its denticulated moulding below the roofline, Corinthian style finials and decorative iron work balcony (18th century).

From the Hôtel de Boisbilly, go down to the Place au Beurre, where once the butter market was held.

Turn right along the rue du Sallé, a good place to study the development of domestic/ commercial architecture, with half-timbered houses from the 16-17th centuries with varying degrees of elaborate decoration, flanking a stone-faced structure from 1800.

At the end of the street, cross over into the narrow rue Treuz (twisted street) which contains straight ahead perhaps the **oldest house in Finistère**, dating back to the beginning of 15th century. It has now been fully restored.

Bear left down steps and through the courtyard to see more evidence of this ancient quarter and then continue up more steps and turn left into **rue des Gentilhommes**.

View from Pont Medard

As the name suggests, this has some impressive houses, such as No.12 with its Ionic pilastered doorway and bull's eye windows and nearby a smart and colourful neighbour with brightly painted *colombage* and slate facing on the upper storey.

Cross the Pont Medard ahead (once a drawbridge and gate into the walled city) over the Steir into the Duke's territory.

To the right is a weir where ducal mills once stood. To the left, note the little turret in the old wall of the *ville close* above the water.

Turn left through the **Place Terre au Duc** with its fine houses from the 16th-18th century, both half-timbered and in stone.

The square tower protruding from one roof once provided a look-out, probably on the old port. Little round markers on buildings bearing the date 2000 mark the height of the Steir's terrible flooding in that year.

Continue ahead along **rue René Madec**.

A painted panel at No.5. shows the eponymous Madec at the height of his career as a nabob in India. He was born in Quimper in 1736 of humble origins, then went to sea and served in India for the Compagnie des Indes. He reached a position of power through service in the private army of the Grand Mogul, before returning to Brittany. He died in 1784 after a fall from his horse.

Go straight ahead to the river Odet and cross on a passerelle.

The hill behind the tourist office is **Mt Frugy**, which offers walking paths and views over the town. According to archaeological evidence, this was an early ritual site. It was later used as a place of execution.

*Take the footpath to the right along the river passing what was once the port area and then follow rue J-B Bousquet to reach the heart of **Locmaria**, the oldest settlement.*

It has been a centre of the pottery industry from pre-Roman times, with local clay abundant down-river. Jean-Baptiste Bousquet revived the practice in 1690, and the works of **Henriot**, with its large shop selling the famous colourful Breton peasant scenes of traditional Quimper pottery, are still operational today. The **Musée de la Faience** illustrates the history of pottery with some stunning examples.

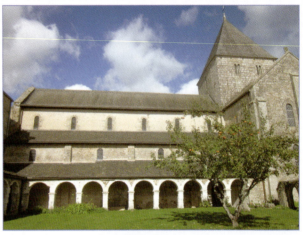

Notre-Dame de Locmaria

The Romanesque architecture of **Notre-Dame de Locmaria** offers a worthy contrast of simplicity with the ornate cathedral. Remains of the 12th century cloister can be seen in the little garden reached by a door in the south aisle. Across the road are riverside medieval-style gardens with labelled plants of medicinal and culinary interest, and seats by the fountain.

Cloisters

Return to the centre by the same route, and cross the river on the same passerelle to reach rue du Parc. Keep on the shop side of this road so as not to miss the entrance to the **Passage de l'Epée** past the café of that name.

This little internal alley - *go right through to regain rue du Parc* - has display windows with interesting old photos, pictures and drawings of Quimper, including scenes during the war and an idea of the cathedral without its spires. Local lace, *coiffes* and musical memorabilia can also be seen. The name comes from the former Hotel de l'Epée here, once an important meeting place for political groups.

On the opposite side of the river is the **Prefecture**. Formerly the hospital of Ste-Catherine, it became the Prefect's administrative headquarters, rebuilt in neo-Renaissance style after being burnt by the Germans on their departure in WII.

Go back a few paces and turn up rue St-François to visit **Les Halles**, the covered market, and then right along **rue Kéréon** with its ancient houses - note one from 1522 on the corner with a statue of Notre-Dames des Portes in a wall niche - and chic shops (famous macaroons), to return to the cathedral square.

Rue Kéréon (Cobblers' Street)

No.5 MENHIR DE KERLOAS   Circular   Grade 2   7.6km

This straightforward walk starts from the tallest standing-stone in France and encircles the highest ridge in the Pays d'Iroise, passing through undulating farmland on tracks and roads where tractors outnumber cars. Long views give glimpses of the Rade de Brest and a constantly changing perspective on this fertile countryside and its dairy farms.

Starting point: Kerloas. From St-Renan take Rue General De Gaulle, direction Le Conquet. About 1km from outskirts of St-Renan turn right (signed Menhir de Kerloas). After 3km park in large lay-by on left.

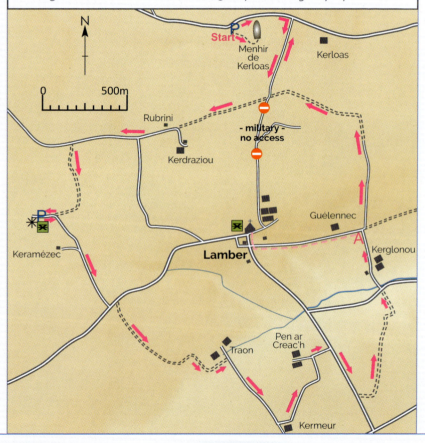

Menhir de Kerloas This is the tallest (upright) Neolithic standing-stone in France at over 9.5m, and it was once considerably larger before the top was lopped off in a storm in the 18th century. The location is on a slight rise, making it visible for more than 30kms. It may have been placed as part of an alignment with other *menhirs* across a wide area as a navigational marker, a boundary stone, signpost and/or a ritual site. It was associated in fairly recent times with fertility: rubbing oneself against the stone's low protuberance was said to make men more likely to have sons and women more likely to be in control of their households... There is an exhibition about the *menhir*, nick-named The Hunchback, in the funerary chapel of the parish church at Plouarzel.

Menhir de Kerloas

Belvedere of Keramézec This view-point has been constructed at the highest point of the ridge (142m). A series of banal questions mark the path of ascent. At the top are an orientation table and pictures of the distant spires visible all around, although it has to be said that wind-farms dominate the sky-line today. It's a good place to pause, with picnic tables and a dry toilet provided.

Diversion to Lamber Although the church of St-Peter (Lamber = lann Ber, holy place of Peter) has been much restored, the simple nave clearly shows its Romanesque origins, with traces of ancient frescoes on a pillar. There is a *fontaine* with a statue of the saint and a fine carved Green Man over the west door. In the cemetery is a monument to the dead with the inscription in Breton urging passers-by to pray for those who gave their lives for God and country. A scenic picnic table is perched on a grassy knoll next to the church.

Green Man at Lamber

DIRECTIONS

A *(Optional) diversion to Lamber, 600m each way. (**Note**: it is not possible to return to the starting point by taking the road directly north from Lamber as this passes through a restricted military area.)*

No.6 ST-DERRIEN   Circular   Grade 2   8.1 or 13.1km

The Flèche here follows its sinuous course through a pastoral wooded valley and the main route meanders alongside it from the pretty lake in St-Derrien. Two mills and a cascade are passed on the way before retracing the outward stretch back to the starting point. The walk can be prolonged by a further (less scenic) circuit around the village..

Starting point: St-Derrien is just north of the D32 between Landivisiau and Lesneven. Park by the *plan d'eau* (lake) near the centre of the village.

St-Derrien The village is named for Derrien, one of the wave of holy men from Wales and Cornwall who came to evangelize Brittany in the Age of Saints (from the 5th-8th centuries). His legend tells of journeying to the Holy Land before returning to western Europe via Nantes. From there he travelled with his companion Néventer overland to Brest, and on the way through this district of Léon dealt with a ferocious monster that was terrorizing the land. The church and *fontaine* are dedicated to him.

St-Derrien, the starting point

DIRECTIONS

A *Turn right up the road and take a small path on the left along a field, just past the driveway of a house.*
B *Turn left over mill race (bridge), then past mill bear right and through buildings to road, but there bear right along path*
C *Ignore path uphill and path left, and turn right along wide path parallel with main road, but above it.*
D *Path splits, ignore one steeply uphill, take other straight on through earth bank, signed Moulin de Lansolot.*
E *Path splits, go left for the extended walk around the village, go right to return to the starting point.*

Mill race at Moulin Lansolot

Moulin de Lansolot Dating from 1646, this mill belonged originally to the nearby Manoir de Kerbrat, before being sold at the time of the Revolution. Working until 2014, it concentrated on the production of *blé noir* (sarrasin) flour.

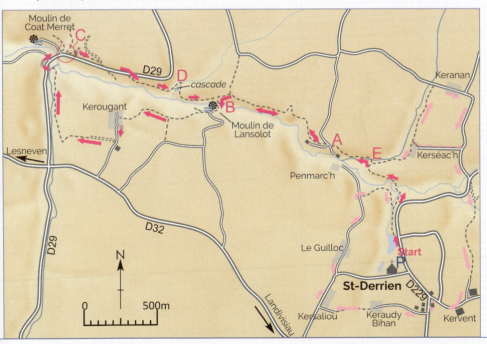

St-Derrien

Moulin de Coat Merret

Moulin de Coat Merret
The earliest elements here date from 1618, but numerous additions and renovations have greatly enlarged the site over time. Many types of flour are still produced here by the Minoterie de Siohan: the family have been in situ since 1850. Guided visits are offered in the summer season.

Cascade The path winds through the trees here to cross the stream (ground may be muddy and stones slippery) and pass beside a series of little cascades before re-approaching the Moulin de Lansolot.

Cascade

No.7 LAMPAUL-GUIMILIAU   Circular   Grade 2   11.1km

The truncated spire of this exceptional church becomes a point of reference as the walk circles the village on rural tracks, with the high point of a former telegraph station hill for long views before descending into the woods of Coat Meur (the great wood) to the sylvan setting of a pretty *fontaine*. The *bourg* itself with some admirable architecture merits further exploration. The Maison de Patrimoine is open at certain times for more local history.

Starting point: Lampaul-Guimiliau, 3.5km SW of Landivisiau on the D11. Park by the church and take the road opposite, D11 to St-Sauveur and Commana, then right on the Rue du Stade (see map).

Église Notre-Dame This is one of the finest parish close churches. As the village name shows, it was once associated with St Pol (Paul Aurelien) and a local saint, Miliau. Outside are the essential elements: an impressive triumphal entrance gate (16th century), ornate ossuary chapel (1667) and rather simple *calvaire*. The tower was built in 1573 and was 70m tall before a lightning strike took the top off in 1809. The interior is well worth visiting for the impressive gilded altarpieces, one portraying the life of St Miliau himself who was decapitated by his brother, a wonderful Baroque baptismal font and many tiny details - look inside the holy water stoup.

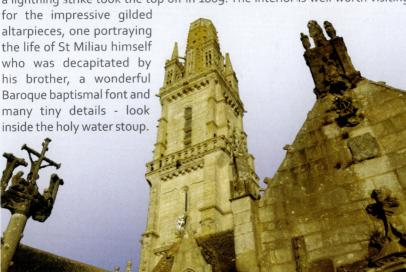

Église Notre-Dame

DIRECTIONS
A *At a fork go left, not right downhill.*
B *Turn left by the calvaire to see the fontaine of St-Pol, then return.*

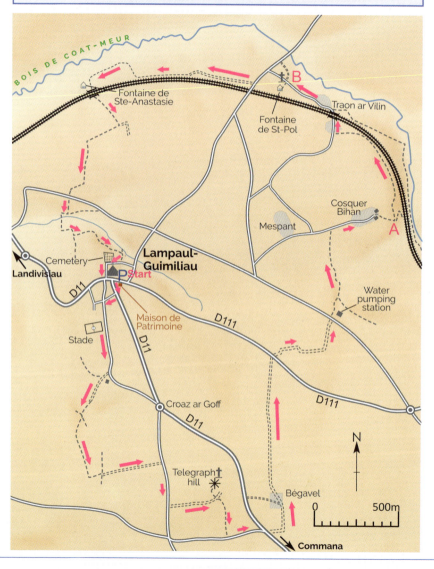

Lampaul-Guimiliau

Télégraphe Chappe
On this spot there was once a pyramid-shaped communications tower, first established in 1798, with mechanical arms to represent numbers or letters according to their position. It was part of a chain of sixty-two stations between Paris and Brest, and continued working until 1852. The system was developed by Claude Chappe in 1794. Each tower had an observation post and sleeping quarters for the operator, as well as the signalling mechanism.

Fine view from the telegraph hill

The Christianization of the site dates to the late 19th century. There is a modern orientation table.

Railway This is the main Paris-Brest line, originally built in the 1860s.

Fontaine de St-Pol There is a statue of the saint wearing a bishop's mitre in the niche above the spring and a foundation stone of 1661, as well as the coat of arms of the Le Sénéchal family. A head of Jesus and instruments of the passion are above.

Fontaine de Ste-Anastasie The legend of Saint Anastasie relates how the young noblewoman who used to pray by this spring was killed by her father, lord of Coat Meur, for refusing marriage in favour of the spiritual life. The *fontaine* structure has the date 1803 and was sponsored by a tanner named Yves Jaffrès.

Fontaine de Ste-Anastasie

No.8 RIBOUL POTIC - history of a landscape
Circular   Grade 2   4.9km

This short route offers the chance to study the development of a section of the Queffleuth valley. It has been established by the Association Au Fil du Queffleuth et de la Penzé, based in Pleyber-Christ (aufilduqueffleuthetdelapenze-over.blog.com), whose purpose is to foster and promote the heritage of the two river valleys named in their title. The information boards are in French, so detailed explanations are given here to help understanding of the economic past and natural habitat of this idyllic spot.

Starting point: Le Peen on the D769 Morlaix-Carhaix. Take the turning to Pleyber-Christ, signed Crêperie des Fougères, and park on the right (see map).

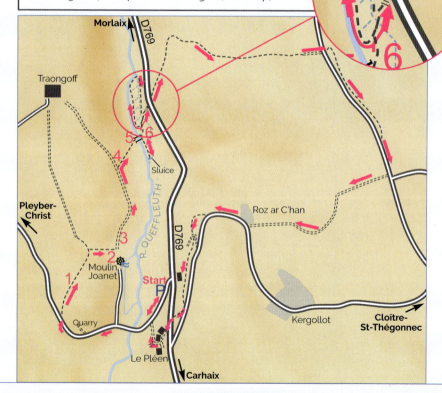

page 44   *Riboul Potic*

The Queffleuth rises on the northern slopes of the Monts d'Arrée near Roc'h Trédudon in the commune of Plouneour-Menez. It meanders along the secluded valley of the ancient Abbaye du Relec, where monks once diverted the water to fish-ponds and mills, before turning north to reach Morlaix, a mere 19kms from source. Here it joins with the Jarlot almost underneath the current Town Hall and together they form the Morlaix river or Dosssen, which runs out into the Channel at Carentec 13kms later. Despite the narrow channel of the Queffleuth, this little river (probably 'a lively stream' in Breton) has the capacity to flood swiftly and the centre of Morlaix has felt its destructive power in very recent times. This potential for disaster is reflected in a legend which claims that a horseman was stationed on the dyke at Le Relec, ready to gallop off and warn the townspeople when water levels began to rise.

Landscape trail

Numerous mills along the course of this river were in industrial use from the 17th to 19th centuries. In addition to traditional flour preparation, cloth production, a local industry of enormous economic importance before the Revolution, also used mill facilities for *teillage* (separation of fibres). The high water quality of the Queffleuth - low in iron and without chalk particles - made it particularly suitable for paper production and as early as 1629 a Norman named Julien Cordier was granted land to build the Moulin de Glaslan, paying part of his rent in reams of paper. It was still operational on a large scale in the 19th century when the Andrieux family developed the business through mechanization, and were socially responsible employers of many locals who had access to a school and subsidised accommodation.

One reason that this particular industry thrived here was the proximity of the Monts d'Arrée, where certain villages - particularly La Feuillée - had developed a tradition of itinerant trade to compensate for the poor quality of their land. The *pilhouaerien* (French *chiffoniers*) or rag-and-bone men travelled extensively and collected large quantities of rags to supply the paper-mills in the Queffleuth valley.

Riboul Potic

Stop 1 Looking across the valley here - not so easy if maize is growing in the field next to the lane - shows how the use of the terrain has changed in the last 150 years. In 1837 there were 65 small parcels of land all enclosed by banks and hedges. Mechanisation of farming from 1960s onwards changed the face of the landscape, and today there are only 9 divisions. The erasure of most of the boundaries has contributed to soil erosion, flooding and pollution of rivers.

Stop 2 The Moulin Jouannet (private property) is the only working mill remaining on the Queffleuth, where a turbine is used to provide domestic electricity. Formerly the valley was a source of flour, fabric and paper production, with mills often changing their function to meet current industrial needs.

Stop 3 A moment to pause and take in the variety of trees which are noted on the board: *saule* (willow), *bouleau* (birch) *chêne* (oak), *if* (yew) and *hêtre* (beech). The densely wooded hillside on the other side of the river is a comparatively recent development. The land would have been under cultivation in the 19th century, but the extensive development of silviculture or wood production in the latter years of that period and the decline of arable farming in the 20th century led to natural re-forestation and the appearance of plantations, such as spruce.

Stop 4 This beautiful sunken way or *chemin creux* was once a common feature of the Breton countryside, although many have now been lost to modern farming expansion and mechanization. The passage has been hollowed out by hundreds of years of foot and hoof fall as the route provided connections between farms, fields and villages. In places the banks were often reinforced by stone walling.

Slab bridge

Riboul Potic

Stop 5 The river was a vital industrial resource especially in the 19th century, with mills producing various commodities, notably paper. Today the Queffleuth is a 1st category fishing course known for salmon and trout and also provides a natural habitat for many other species of animal (otters and king-fishers, for example) and plants such as the Royal Fern (*osmunda regalis*).

Stop 6 The stone bridge is an ancient crossing-point, possibly dating back to Gallo-Romano times. This part of the valley had a specific irrigation system to keep the water-meadow (*prairie*) humid and in condition for pasture or hay production.

A channel (*bief*) was taken off the river course (the *vanne* or regulating valve can still be seen a little way upstream to the right) where it meandered around the boundary of the field and rejoined at the far end. Irrigation channels (see map inset) were dug across the *prairie* in a 'fish-bone' pattern to distribute the water to all parts in times of low rainfall. When the river was high, the land acted as a sponge to help prevent wider flooding. The prairie also absorbed some of the effects of pollution before run-off water from the hillsides reached the river.

Prat ar Gaor The notice-boards of this mini-circuit around the Prat ar Gaor (Goat Meadow) use the character of Potic, a *pilhaouer* or rag-man, to explain the original uses of the meadow, how it was maintained and harvested, originally by hand using a scythe, from the 19th century right up to 1980. After being cut for hay up until 2005 it fell into disuse until becoming a grazing area for horses.

This site is one of great biodiversity. Newts, frogs, whirligig water beetles and large red damsel flies profit from the rapid flow of the river. The meadow itself acts as a sponge in times of heavy rainfall, first holding then later releasing its moisture in dryer times. It also provides a natural filter to mitigate the effects of nitrate and phosphate pollution.

The walking circuit now continues across the main road (D769), climbing steeply through woodland to a height with good views over the countryside. A raised path in the trees then runs alongside a minor road until a junction where the first of a series of well-signed footpaths re-descends to the valley to complete this attractive short rural walk.

> **In the vicinity** It's also worth visiting the Musée du Loup (Wolf Museum) in nearby Le Cloître St-Thégonnec, and the Romanesque Abbaye du Relec.

No.9 HUELGOAT   Circular   Grade 2   12.1km

This is a walk of two halves. The first passes by some of the most famous sites in the forest, both natural wonders and man-made creations, whilst the second is a rural ramble in the leafy countryside outside the town. A final stretch alongside the lake offers a new perspective of the *bourg* across the water.

Starting point: parking area near supermarket, Route de Berrien, Huelgoat (see map). After visiting Le Champignon, cross the Route de Berrien and follow the track ahead.

Directions
A *On reaching the Chaos continue ahead following the line of the river.*
B *Fork right down to Mare aux Sangliers and cross bridge. Continue up steps to turn left at the top.*
C *At a junction of tracks and paths take the path to the right. The track to the left ahead offers a short-cut to the starting point.*
D *Cross the swimming pool carpark to find the footbridge over the river, then continue on path between river and road.*

Le Champignon (Mushroom) Just opposite the parking area, perched on a small hill, is a mushroom-shaped granite boulder of enormous proportions.

La Roche Tremblante (Trembling Rock) This rock, like the Mushroom, has been made conspicuous by isolation, the result of intensive quarrying of granite here in the late 19th century. The centre of operations was where the bar/crêperie by the Trembling Rock now stands, and lingering evidence can be seen in the marks of stone-cutting tools on some lower rocks in this area. The Trembling Rock (over 100 tons) itself has a line of chisel holes across the top. It is possible to make the whole mass rock gently if pressure is applied in the perfect spot…

Relic of quarrying activity

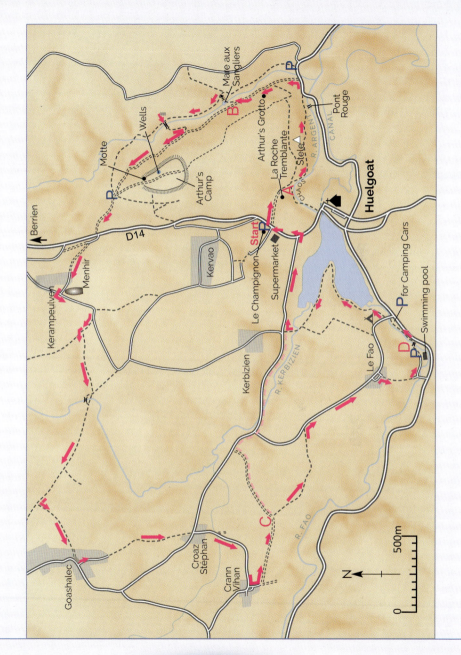

Chaos The magnificent granite Chaos of gigantic boulders tumbling down the deep valley of the river Argent is the result of volcanic movement 350 million years ago when magma was forced up slowly from deep beneath the earth. Cooling over aeons, the mass then cracked and was gradually rounded into boulders by the penetration of water over another long period of time. Eventually, the pile toppled and rolled into the extraordinary profusion of shapes and formations in existence today. The water continues to flow deep beneath the rocks. The Chaos was threatened by quarrying activity, but a campaign by the Touring Club of France and others saw this part of the forest purchased by the commune in 1903 and the site protected. Today the most famous part is called Le Ménage de la Vièrge, or the Virgin's Household Utensils because - apparently - some rocks resemble a cradle, saucepan, bed, etc.

Chaos, Ménage de la Vièrge

Stele A plaque on the wall gives the names of three young resistance fighters whose bodies were found on the hillside here in early 1946. They were shot and buried by the Germans in July 1944. On the slope high above, a granite stele records their loss.

Pont Rouge The old slab bridge to the right of the path is of uncertain age, with estimates ranging from Celtic times to the medieval period.

Arthur's Grotto This magnificent cave is a natural formation, associated later (maybe as late as the 1970s) with King Arthur as a tourist attraction. Its evocative appearance makes an easy association with the spot where Arthur is supposed to lie awaiting a national emergency worthy of resuscitation. Arthur certainly has strong legendary links with Brittany, some more convincing than others.

Mare aux Sangliers The name of Wild Boars' Pool may be purely prosaic as a drinking-place for the animal that has always been an inhabitant of this forest. Some prefer imaginative links, connecting the shape of the rocks with the heads of wild boar...

Arthur's Camp The steep hill to the left of the path was once topped by a genuine Iron Age hill-fort. The Arthur connection is again tenuous. The site was excavated in 1938 by Sir Mortimer Wheeler, who discovered evidence of a *murus Gallicus*, the Celtic defensive method described by Julius Caesar. This involved using tree-trunks in closely-packed stepped formation to secure the hillside. The hill-top was defended by the Osismes, the local Celtic tribe, against the Romans. An idea of the earthwork fortifications and natural rock barriers creating this large camp can still be gained today, and the site of wells, essential in times of siege, can be seen. There is a much later medieval *motte* at the northern entrance. To reach the camp, turn left uphill in the parking area ahead.

Menhir de Kerampeulven A fine standing-stone from the late Neolithic period, now a lone upright but with sizeable companions lying in the earth. It may once have been part of a large alignment with the other single *menhirs* in the Huelgoat area.

Menir de Kerampeulven

The Lake This was created at the end of the 16th century by German engineers to serve the needs of the lead/silver mines near Locmaria-Berrien. A small canal (still flowing in part) carried water over 5km through the forest to drive pumping machinery and to wash minerals. The 15 hectare lake is fed by the Kerbizien and the Fao, and fishing is allowed with a permit from the *mairie*.

Huelgoat and lake

No.10 GOUÉZEC   Circular   Grade 2/3   5.5km

From the village this walk climbs steadily to a lofty ridge offering an exceptional vantage point over central Finistère. To reach the highest peak of rock and the best views, an upward scramble and descent requiring care are necessary, but there is a lower alternative on a regular path for those who wish to avoid such challenges.
Allow plenty of time to enjoy the panorama.

Starting point: Park by the church in centre of Gouézec (see map).

Directions
A *Take the straight earth path to left between banks, cross over wooden bridge and continue up through wood, then more open heath. Keep moving up towards the ridge.*
B *Bear left when path joins from right, then leave it to bear right up into grassy field and cross it.*
C *At the Roche du Feu the path divides: right for rocky scramble over top, left for easier route to other side.*
D *Through carpark, cross road to picnic area. Here bear right to far end to find broad path downhill.*

The church of St-Peter was built in the 16th century with a good deal of remodelling in the succeeding centuries. The triumphal entrance gate with its statues in dark Kersanton (favoured stone of sculptors) dates from 1754. Inside there is a fine stained glass window (1571) behind the high altar.

Roche du Feu (Karreg an Tan in Breton) This rocky pinnacle gets its name 'Rock of Fire' from a warning beacon said to have been lit here during Viking raids up the Aulne. It was third in a chain starting at the mouth of the Aulne estuary and then on the top of Menez Hom. The earliest Breton name of this rocky outcrop was Menez-Gu, which could be a mutation of Menez-Ku, a place of refuge.

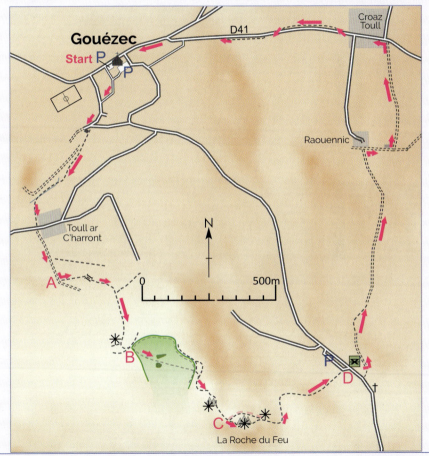

The '*dolmen*' (stone table in Breton) is not a genuine neolithic monument - it was erected in 1963 using stone from a quarry at Pont Coblant and once had a round compass (outline visible) on the flat rock.

Panorama The view north over the Aulne valley shows rich farmland, in contrast to the thin, acidic soil of the Monts d'Arrée area beyond, where the peak of Mont-St-Michel-de-Brasparts with its little chapel on the summit is visible. To the north-west rise the distinctive heights of Menez Hom and the Montagne de Locronan can be seen to the south-west.

> The Montagnes Noires (black mountains, Menez Du in Breton) are a range of hills running east-west across central Finistère. The culmination is Menez Hom (330m), an impressive high point at the start of the Crozon peninsula. They are made up of schist, quartzite and Armorican *grès*, and were an important source of slate from the fifteenth to the twentieth century (for example, see p.131 and p.135). The name 'Black Mountains' probably comes from this, but it could also be a reference to their densely wooded slopes. The Roche du Feu is one of the highest viewpoints.

View north across the Aulne valley to the Monts d'Arrée

> The Nantes-Brest Canal runs through the valley below.
> For another walk nearby see the **Nantes-Brest Canal** feature.
> Walk No.4 starts at **Pont Coblant**, just 3km to the north of Gouézec.
> (See p.135)

No.11 LOCRONAN — Circular — Grade 2 — 8.1km

This rural circuit gives a good idea of the beautiful, wooded landscape in which Locronan, the holy place of St Ronan, stands. The village itself, dominated by a fine church and chapel, has a curious dual personality: its picturesque 17th century heart has been in great demand as a film-set and created a significant tourist destination, and yet the early history of a Celtic religious site and the figure of St Ronan himself lend a more indefinable quality. On the route, long views of the distinctive three humps of Menez Hom, the Crozon peninsula and the sea in the Bay of Douarnenez all add to the appeal.

Starting point: centre of Locronan. Facing the church, take the street from the far left corner of the square and turn left immediately down steep narrow alley signed Chapelle de Bonne-Nouvelle (see map).

St Ronan This Breton saint of Irish origin is said to have arrived to evangelize Brittany in the early 6th century, although he soon antagonised the local women on the Bay of Douarnenez by attempting to stop the wrecking of passing boats, and had to move on inland to the Bois du Nevet. He created his hermitage on the site of an earlier Celtic/Druidic *nemeton* or ritual space, aligned to the movements of the heavens, with twelve special points echoing twelve zodiacal months and twelve pagan deities. It is said that once a week the saint, barefooted, followed the full 12km boundary of this area in prayer and contemplation.

Settling in the Bois du Nevet did not put an end to his problems, however: a woman named Keben accused Ronan of making away with her daughter, and although he proved his innocence to King Gradlon (see p.28) and brought the girl back from the dead, the mother continued a campaign of harassment against him. Scenes from Ronan's life, including Keben's hostility, appear in medallions on the pulpit (1707) in the church.

Église de St-Ronan

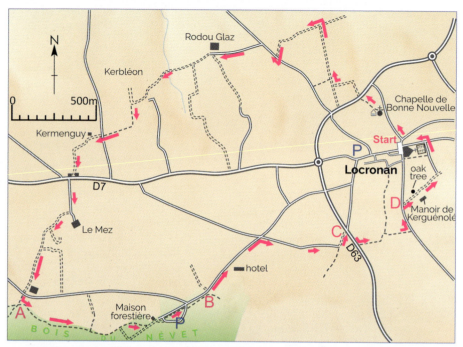

Place de l'Église

Directions

A *About 70m after leaving road, turn left through gap in wall into wood and follow wide track along fence. (Other walk options posssible, see page 58, Bois du Névet)*

B *Rejoin road through gap in bank before path turns right down into wood.*

C *At the main road, D63, beware fast traffic. Ignore road opposite, turn right on main road and go along verge to take track on left after about 150m.*

D *Turn in through stone posts of manoir, go ahead past symbolic oak. At next stone posts turn left downhill.*

Locronan sits below its 'mountain' and between the two forested areas, the Bois du Duc and the Bois du Névet. The village owes much of its refined architecture to wealth from the manufacture of sailcloth, an industry which flourished here especially in the 16th and 17th centuries, when the finished product was shipped abroad from Pouldavid near Douarnenez. Shakespeare refers to this fabric in Coriolanus (Act II, Scene 1) describing a kitchen-maid pinning her 'lockram' around her neck. The village remains well-known as a centre of crafts with many workshops and retail outlets today. The imposing Église de St-Ronan dates from the 15th century, with the attached Chapelle de Penity, said to be on the site of Ronan's tomb, added in 1530. A statue and a 15th century version of the tomb in Kersanton stone portray the saint.

The pretty chapel of **Notre-Dame de Bonne-Nouvelle** with its *calvaire* dates from the late 15th century, with later renovations. The bell-tower is probably contemporary with the elaborate *fontaine* behind (1698), a source of public water, which was paid for by a wealthy cloth merchant. The stained-glass windows in the chapel are from 1985.

Chapelle de Notre Dame de Bonne-Nouvelle

The **Manoir de Kerguénolé** was built in 1907 as a cultural centre. In the grounds is the Chêne du Névet, an oak tree planted in 2007, a symbolic reminder of the pagan past of the forest, the importance of trees in the environment and their role in the preservation of life on the planet.

Petite and Grande Troménie Each year in July a special walk is held here, an echo of St Ronan's ambulatory worship in the surrounding countryside. The Petite Troménie is only 4km, but every six years the Grande Troménie (next 2019) covers the full 12km of the *nemeton*. The event attracts huge crowds of participants and combines spiritual and festive aspects.

View towards Menez Hom

Bois du Névet

This 225 hectare wood of beautiful oak and beech trees was once the site of a Druidic *nemeton* or sacred space. Later legends speak of secret underground passages and buried treasure. The wood is criss-crossed by walking, cycling and riding paths. Our walk only touches the northern edge. From this point of entry (marked A on the map), turn right or go straight ahead to explore further. The Hent Kreiz (central road), where the *Maison forestière* passed on our route is situated, runs right across the middle of the wood, making a good navigational tool.

No.12 SCAËR — Circular — Grade 2 — 7.5km

This is a beautiful country walk, mostly through woods and along enclosed tracks, ending with a glorious stretch of river bank along the Isole. An imposing standing-stone offers a mid-way focal point, but the overall experience of trees, flowers, butterflies and birdsong is a worthy end in itself.

Starting point: Chapelle Ste-Thérèse at Cascadec. From centre of Scaër take the D782 eastwards, cross the river Isole and at a roundabout turn right onto the D6 to St-Thurien. After 200m at a left hand right-angle bend, turn off right (ahead) and continue ahead following the river for 2km, fork left (don't cross bridge) and park (see map).

Valley of Isole This river rises in the Montagnes noires and finally joins the Ellé at Quimperlé 22km to the south of this walk. The deep valley here provides a beautiful end to the route, with the exceptionally clear waters dancing around granite rocks in the river-bed and tumbling down cascades. It is very popular for trout-fishing.

Chapelle de Ste Thérèse The walk starts near this abandoned chapel with ornate doorway and bell-tower, standing rather forlornly near the river Isole. It was originally situated in the commune of Scrignac in the Monts d'Arrée, but the dilapidated remains were sold in 1926 to an industrial magnate who reconstructed it on this spot to serve the workers at the nearby paper factory.

River Isole

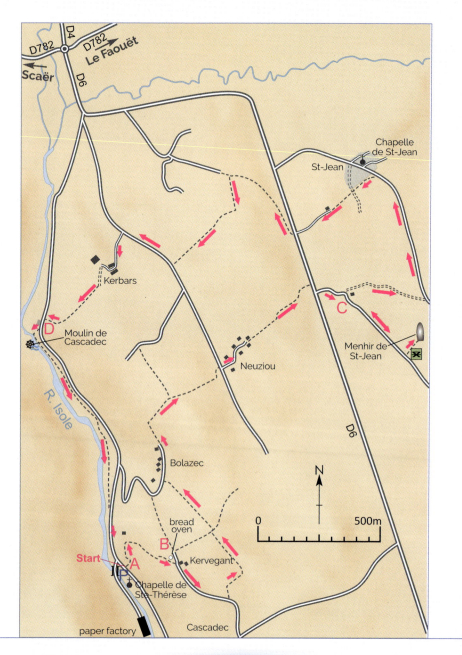

Directions

A Over the road from the parking area, take the footpath into the trees and uphill.
B Possible short-cut to Bolazec via footpath straight on from end of road.
C Detour via road to the Menhir de St-Jean (good place for a picnic) and return.
D At the road, bear left to a path on opposite side, down to riverside.

Menhir de St-Jean

Bread oven In the hamlet of Kervegant look out for this particularly good example of a communal *four à pain*, once used by villagers to bake their bread.

Menhir de St-Jean This is an impressive stone, 7m high, and possibly once part of a larger Neolithic alignment. The rural environment is attractive and a picnic-table provides a good resting-point.

Chapelle de St-Jean Once associated with the Knights of St-John, the order of '*hospitalier*' monks, this large chapel dates from the 16-17th century.

The remains of the **Moulin de Cascadec** are an indication of the industrial past of this valley. Originally a flour mill, it came into the ownership of paper-makers named Faugeyroux, in about 1830. A factory for production was built further downstream, fed by a canal. In 1893 the site was rented by Réné-Guillaume Bolloré, who won a gold medal for his cigarette-paper products at the Universal Exhibition in Paris in 1900. His son took over and bought the site in 1917. The family's successful manufacturing enterprise (together with an original plant on the Odet at Ergué-Gabéric near Quimper) employed a large workforce (700 at Cascadec in 1930). The OCB (Odet-Cascadec-Bolloré) brand of cigarette-papers became famous. The factory was state-of-the-art for its time, but a chemical engineer who visited in 1925 said that while the Isole was charming, the isolation was not! Today the factory is still in operation, part of the Glatfelter group, producing a range of items from coffee filters to surgical masks.

No.13 ROCHES DU DIABLE   Circular   Grade 2   6.5km

This walk starts with an up-close view of the Devil's Rocks before a rural tour to reach the opposite bank of the river and look down on the spectacle from a lofty viewpoint. Some road walking joins pretty wooded paths, former mill-workings and watery scenery.

Starting point: Les Roches du Diable, signed from the centre of Locunolé, which is 10km NE of Quimperlé. (See map).

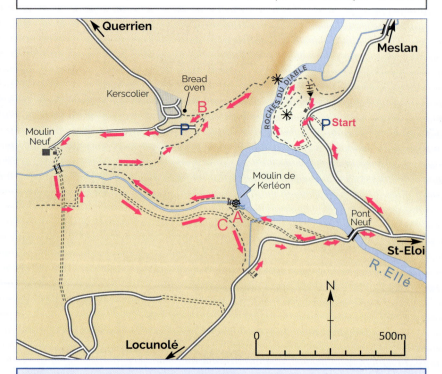

Directions

A *Bear left of mill and cross the stream. Turn left on the other side.*
B *Divert a few paces here to see four à pain (bread oven).*
C *Possible option to return to the mill to shorten the walk.*

Les Roches du Diable

Roches du Diable Devil's Rocks is the name given to a dramatic granite Chaos of huge, oddly shaped boulders in the Ellé river, which flows through an imposing gorge at this point. The inevitable legend concerns St Guenolé (the nearby village is called Locunolé = holy place of Guenolé) who established his hermitage here, but the Devil became jealous of his success in converting souls to Christianity and tried to bury the saint in a mountain of rocks. Guenolé made the sign of the cross and was saved and the rocks remained scattered on the river bed. The Devil was forced to hurl himself into a fathomless hole beneath the waters of the river.

Pont Neuf This mid 19th century bridge was constructed on the site of a much older crossing. This point marks the boundary of the territories of the bishops of Quimper and Vannes.

Moulin de Kerléon Now missing its wooden mill-wheels, this mill was in business up until the 1970s. Part of a quern is propped against the wall. The original building probably dates back to the end of the 15th century, and once belonged to the lord of a nearby manor (Coativy) which no longer exists.

Kerscolier There is a large village bread-oven in this hamlet on the way to the viewpoint over the gorge.

No.14 RIEC-sur-BELON   Circular   Grade 2   5.3km

A peaceful walk beside the waters of this multi-armed estuary, with the simple pleasures of light on the water, boating activity, an impressive mill building and a riverside chapel.

Starting point: Lannéguy, 3km due south of Riec-sur-Belon. From the carpark, turn sharp left before the 'No-through-road' sign and walk down to the *fontaine* and Chapelle de St-Leger (see map).

Chapelle de St-Léger Curiously, this building was formed in the 19th century from two earlier chapels close together on this spot, one dedicated to St Léger, who was invoked especially by parents who had a lame child, and the other to Notre-Dame de Grâces. The stream of the existing elaborate 17th century *fontaine* ran between the chapels. There is a picnic table behind the chapel with views of the estuary.

Belon The estuary is most famous for its oysters, said to have a distinctive nutty flavour. It is also a haven for mud

Chapelle de St-Léger

and marsh-loving birds at low tide. It's not impossible that you might see the large duck named the Tadorne de Belon, with distinctive colouring of green (head and neck), white, russet (band round chest) and black (stripe on wings). It is actually named after Pierre Belon, a 16th century naturalist.

Moulin Edouard This handsome building, now private property, was a working flour mill until the 1960s. It has three wheels and a 12m cascade.

A short detour can be made here to a tiny *fontaine* perched up on the hillside. The carefully created stone basin is a reminder of the importance of water sources, however humble, in Christian and pre-Christian faith.

Lannéguy The Boulangerie des Chaumières is an organic bakery on the route in this hamlet. It's hard to miss the beautiful eponymous thatched houses.

Head of the creek, Anse de Penmor

Directions

A Divert a few paces to the left here for a fine viewpoint over the estuary.

B If time permits, follow this beautiful wooded path down the estuary and then return.

C Either retrace outward route or, for variety, follow this heathland path.

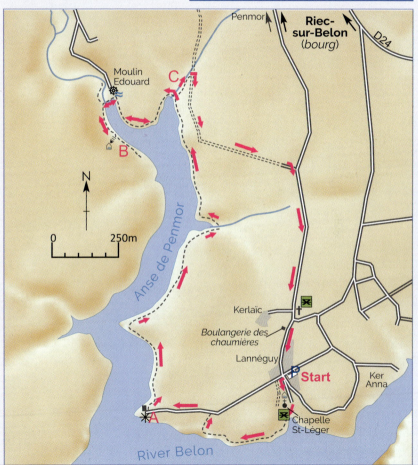

No.15 PLOBANNALEC   Circular   Grade 1   6km

This level walk on quiet roads through fairly open countryside and rural hamlets passes several Neolithic sites including the remarkable remains at Quélarn. History-lovers will not be disappointed, but it offers a pleasantly un-taxing route for everyone.

Starting point: Letty Vraz (see map), 3.5km from Le Guilvinec via D153 to Treffiagat, turning right there to Plobannalec on 'Route du Letty'. Park on roadside

Directions
A *Follow road round to right (look for sign written on barn) and then left (also signed 'sentier') behind barn on very narrow path.*
B *A small path wiggles through the wood to pass another megalithic site.*

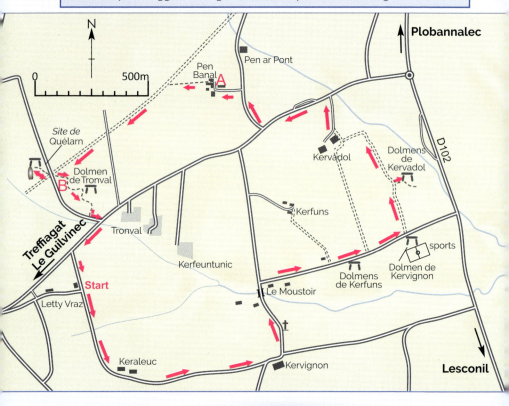

Dolmens de Kerfuns The area is incredibly rich in neolithic monuments. This neglected megalithic site right by the roadside seems to contain remains of several dolmens, possibly once covered by a cairn (see Quélarn below).

Dolmen de Kervignon This dolmen is on the edge of the sports ground and can be accessed over a high grassy bank or through a neighbouring field entrance. Not enough remains of this burial site to give a clear picture of the structure, but this is probably the entrance to a corridor leading to the chamber, like others in the area.

Dolmen de Kervignon

Dolmens de Kervadol Two dolmens close together here may once have been part of a larger conglomeration. The site was certainly used for a long time: the extraordinary Celtic stele showing four gods now on display in the excellent Musée départmentale in Quimper was found here.

Quélarn This major site was first excavated by Paul du Chatellier in 1887. The famous archaeologist Pierre-Roland Giot, a pioneer of scientific methodology, made a detailed study from 1979 to 1983. His work indicates that a 50m cairn once covered a line of compartmented dolmens, each with its own entrance and access corridor. Some of these can be clearly discerned today, other traces are less easy to envisage. There is also a small standing-stone on the site, probably a later addition. The sheer scale of the remains is memorable.

Dolmen de Tronval The 'stone table' effect is clear on this site, with one massive capstone still raised on its supports and another on the ground. It was presumably once part of the Quélarn emplacements.

Quélarn

Megaliths

The earliest form of New Stone Age monuments (from c4800BC onwards) are burial sites. The term **dolmen** ('table of stone' in Breton) was first used in this context in the 18th century by the famous soldier/antiquarian, Théophile-Malo Corret de la Tour d'Auvergne (see page 26). It describes the skeleton of a Neolithic tomb structure, where two uprights supported a lintel or capstone around a burial chamber. The earliest sites were simple passage graves with a short or long stone-lined corridor leading to a round or rectangular inner 'room' where bones or urns could be placed with ritual objects, like weapons, jewellery or food items. Later developments in shape included the *allée couverte* (see p.91 & 122), a type common in Brittany, and buttressed tombs with no roof stones. It is thought that the tombs were then covered with earth so they blended into the landscape, rather than protruded as the exposed remains do today. Sometimes graves were covered with a carapace of small stones in the form known as a cairn. These could contain multiple burial chambers. The finest example of this, and one of the earliest structures in Europe, is in Finistère, at Barnenez (near Walk 17).

A later development was the erection of **menhirs** (Breton for long stones), standing stones which often marked earlier burial sites either singly or in rows called alignments. Their significance is not known with any certainty but they may have been boundary markers, signposts or ceremonial structures, depending on the environmental context.

In the vicinity

This particularly fine example of a menhir can be found nearby behind the dunes at Léhan (near Léchiagat) on the south coast, 3.5km from Quélarn.

Menhir de Léhan

COAST - INTRODUCTION

Château de Dinan (see page 100)

With almost 750km of coast-line and coastal path to choose from in Finistère, it seems helpful to pick out some of the most interesting and impressive locations for walking by the sea in linear fashion, as well as the conventional circular routes. Together these offer variety of terrain from lonely treks on high cliffs to easy walking on fairly level paths, and variety of interest with treats for bird and nature lovers, lighthouses and coastal defences for history buffs and the memorable sight and sound of the ever-changing sea for everybody. Famous and easily accessible landmarks like the Pointe du Raz will of course also offer terrific scenery, but you will probably have to share it with many others, so the selection here is intended to introduce visitors to the best less well-known paths.

The north coast is generally easy going with low headlands and plenty of beaches. It should be noted that this Channel coast has a long tide recoil with resultant large exposed areas of mud and sand at low tide - great for *peche à pied*, of course, where you can search for shellfish for your supper in the sand and rock pools. The first linear suggestion (Meneham) is simply the best place for a seaside stroll here and maybe a swim, combined with a visit of historic interest, something that all the family could enjoy without walking any great distance. Otherwise there are long and short circuits to enjoy some impressive rock formations.

The western Atlantic coast is much more dramatic, often with high cliffs and demanding paths plunging up and down between deep coves and long beaches. The selected sections given as linear walks are up to 10km so that an out and back excursion will give a day's occupation and some serious exercise for the knees. There are easier options for circular walks too, of varying distances, including Penmarc'h (with its very famous lighthouse) on the south-west tip of Brittany and a close-up experience of the Rade de Brest on the Pointe de Doubidy.

For a quintessential and undemanding coastal experience, try some gentle exercise at the pretty little harbour of Doëlan on the southern coast, with its twin lighthouses, sailing and fishing activity, seafood restaurants and low rocky headlands.

The coast offers a very different perspective according to direction and tide-times, making a return later on the same coastal path as good an incentive as the outward route in many cases. For single direction walking, it is also possible to arrange for a lift or a taxi. My advice is to organize this in the morning to the end point and then walk back to your car or accommodation to give more flexible timings. Sometimes it may be possible to take a bus back from the final destination (see Le Conquet, for example). Note that there is more public transport around coastal resorts in the summer season.

> Little booklets of tide-times (*Les horaires de marée*) are available from all press outlets and some coastal bars, a useful tool for planning your walks, or consult the website **www.horaire-maree.fr** in advance.

Doëlan (see page 96)

No.16 LOCQUIREC   Circular   Grade 2   15.3km

This varied coast and inland walk evolves around the laid-back port of Locquirec, in its glorious peninsula setting, surrounded by nine sandy beaches. The route covers spectacularly beautiful rugged coastline and the pretty little town itself before passing along the Douron estuary with glimpses of a Roman bath-house across the water. A final cross-country section through undulating terrain includes hamlets and two contrasting chapels.

Starting point: car-park at Moulin de la Rive on the D64 from Lanmeur to Locquirec (see map).

Beach at Moulin de la Rive

Moulin de la Rive The beach here has some of the oldest rocks in France at the western end. These remnants of granitic gneiss date back about two billion years. An example in the form of a stele is displayed in a town car-park (see map). Some of the natural bank of pebbles fringing this beach were lost during WWII, ground down to make concrete for the Germans' Atlantic Wall defences. The mill (*moulin*) itself dates back to the 17th century and was owned by the local lord. He took a fee from all the locals who were of course obliged to grind their grain here.

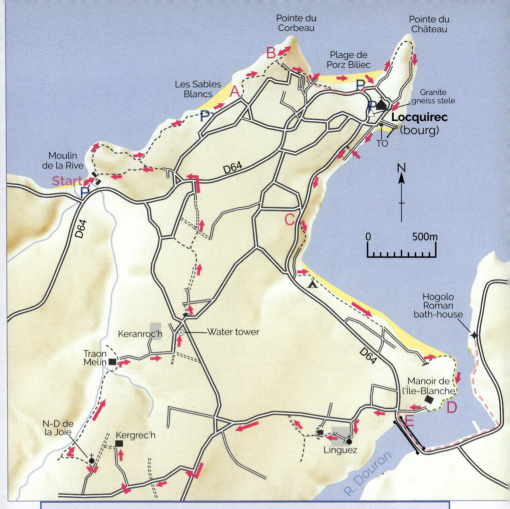

DIRECTIONS

A *Go up to far corner of grassy area to find path leaving from the corner of the road.*

B *Continue to the Pointe du Corbeau for views and then return, turning left past houses to descend.*

C *Ignore paths down to shore until this path, the Chemin de la Falaise.*

D *Alternative path through grounds of Manoir de l'Île Blanche permitted at high tide only.*

E *Divert over bridge here and follow coastal path to see Roman baths.*

Pointe du Château

Pointe du Château An information board here gives details of the quarrying of Locquirec's distinctive bluey-green schist, a stone used in many local buildings.

Église de St-Jacques Originally dedicated to the evangelizing monk Guirec who came to Brittany in the 6th century (and for whom the town is named), the church, thanks to the Knights of St-John, later came under the patronage of St Jacques (of Compostela fame), whose statue - sporting the pilgrim symbol of a scallop shell - looks down from the stair turret beside the church tower (1634). Locquirec was a stage on the trail for travellers from England. A modern stele by the churchyard entrance reminds pilgrims that they only have 1927km to go...

Port Locquirec provides sheltered harbour for pleasure boats and is also well-known as a bathing centre, with a festive race across the bay for swimmers every August. A market is held in the port area on Wednesdays.

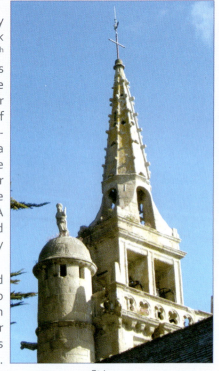
St Jacques

The port

Manoir de Île blanche The manor house here dates from the 17th century but was greatly extended and updated by the wife of Eardley Norton, a lawyer of the Viceroy of India, who bought it in 1903. The cost of the aggrandizement led him to sell up and it became and remains the property of a religious order. It is now used for conferences and spiritual retreats.

Roman bath-house at Hogolo Across the water, this monument with a hypocaust heating system dates from the 1st century AD with later modifications. It lies on the coastal path - allow 40 minutes total for the diversion.

Chapelle de Notre-Dame de Linguez This plain chapel with its simple *calvaire* was founded in the 16th century on the site of a monk's hermitage. Despite various subsequent renovations, it has fallen into disrepair and was in the course of restoration at the time of writing. The intention is to open it for cultural and religious events.

Chapelle de N-D de Linguez

Chapelle de Notre-Dame des Joies This remote-feeling chapel sits in a stately stone enclosure. It dates from the 16th and 17th centuries, but is on the site of an earlier foundation dating back to the period of the Crusades. The interior is highly decorated with paintings on wooden-clad walls and medieval statuary. A simple stepped *calvaire* is outside the precinct, which provides a quiet spot for a rest.

No.17 DOURDUFF-EN-MER   Circular   Grade 2   7.5km

A very varied and beautiful circuit in any season, following the coast of the Bay of Morlaix, verdant rural paths, the centre of a pretty *bourg* and the wooded estuary of the Dourduff, which means 'black water' in Breton.

Starting point: from Morlaix take the D76 northwards, continuing alongside the river for 5 km to cross the bridge over the Dourduff and turn left immediately to reach the parking area (see map).

View across the Bay of Morlaix towards Carantec, Île Louët and the Château du Taureau

Dourduff-en-Mer The coastal starting point was once an important boat-building area: the famous Cordelière, a 700 ton, 200 canon ship built in 1505 for Anne, Duchess of Brittany, began its illustrious career here. In a well-known episode from rivalry between England and France at sea, it was sunk - together with The Regent - with all hands in 1512 off the Pointe St-Mathieu near Brest. The Breton name An Treiz (by bridge) means a crossing place: a ferry was in operation until the road bridge superseded one built for the railway in the 1930s.

Château du Taureau In the bay off Carantec lies this distinctive rocky fortress. It was built in 1544 to deter further raids up the Morlaix river after a disastrous English attack in 1522. It later became a political prison and a place of incarceration for mentally disturbed aristocrats. It was occupied by the Germans in WWII before private occupation saw lavish society parties and a sailing school followed by a final reversion of identity to classified historic monument status. It has been restored and can be visited by boat from Carantec or Plougasnou. See **www.chateaudutaureau.com** for details.

Directions

A *Immediately after some rubbish bins, turn left down a very narrow rocky path.*

B *Follow through houses then take the narrow footpath left just before the first house ahead.*

C *Go through churchyard to right of church and down steps to little road.*

D *Turn right up steps onto another path and follow it down to the water.*

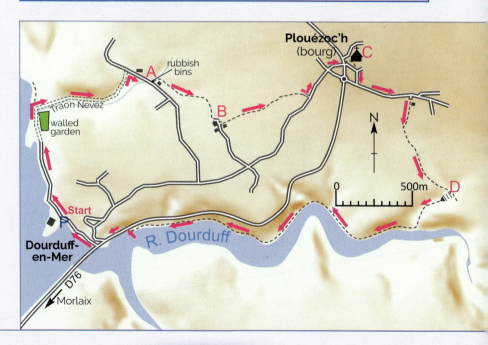

Dourduff-en-Mer

Ile Louët A lighthouse was built on this tiny island in 1857 by Victor Fenoux, the engineer best known for the great viaduct in Morlaix.

Traon Nevez (New Valley) Extending uphill past a large walled garden, this lovely, peaceful valley has been endowed with various works of 'natural art' and simple games. In summer there are also exhibitions.

Plouezoc'h The *bourg* has a bakery and small supermarket, as well as an attractive church. The Église St-Etienne is mainly 17th century with a bell-tower (and typical stair turret) by the famous Beaumanoir school of Morlaix. In the churchyard are two interesting crosses: one a simple monolithic version which is early medieval, and the other a magnificent and unusual wheel-headed 'Hosanna' cross from the 16th century.

'Hosanna' cross

Dourduff estuary

No.18 ST-MICHEL   Circular   Grade 1   5km

A short, easy walk on this low coastline of dramatic rock formations, with places of historic interest on the route from an appealing chapel and oratory to a medieval cemetery and seaweed ovens. There's the opportunity to add a stroll on the beach or a linear extension to an ancient fortification (adding 6.5km).

Starting point: parking on the D32 at Penn Énez, 3km north of Plouguerneau (see map).

Directions

A *Start around the peninsula of Penn Énez, then follow the route inland from the carpark.*

Penn Enez This little peninsula has long association with the seaweed industry, and some old ovens in the ground (for burning the harvest into blocks of sodium carbonate) can still be seen on the higher ground. There is also a guard-house from about 1700, now restored, which was used as a custom-officers' look-out in the 19th century. The contemporary sculptures are by François Breton.

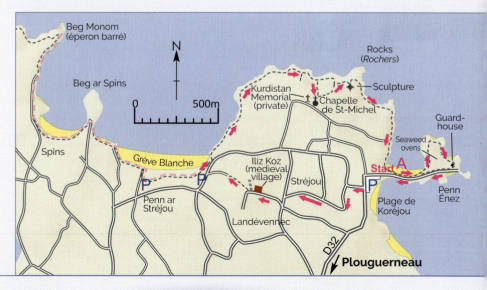

St-Michel

Iliz Koz This 'old church' of the lost parish of Tremenac'h was discovered 5m down in 1969 when a bull-dozer was clearing the land for a house to be built. The church was abandoned in 1729 as the constant encroachment of sand, a major problem on this part of the coast over hundreds of years, became unstoppable. Legend says it was buried as a punishment for miscreants presenting a cat for baptism to the blind old priest... The graveyard contains some medieval tombs with carvings, such as that of a knight with shield, and a cloth merchant.

Iliz Koz

Grève Blanche This pretty beach can add an extra element to the walk, or extend it further on the coastal path to visit Beg Monom, the distinctive round blob of rock on the near horizon. This *éperon barré* or fortified peninsula dates back to the Bronze and Iron Ages, a basic defence system of banks and ditches, using the natural rock formations to protect a central stronghold in times of crisis. Also visible is Île Vierge, the tallest off-shore lighthouse in Europe at 82.5m. The original, dwarfed beside it, dates from 1845, but the greater work took five years to complete (1897-1902). At times it is possible to visit by boat (from Lilia) and climb the 400 internal steps.

Grève Blanche and Beg Monom in the distance

Chapelle de St Michel Take a diversion of 150m off the coastal path to see the chapel dedicated to the archangel Michael. The little oratory commemorates the hermitage of his namesake, famous local priest Michel Le Nobletz, who passed a year on the spot in 1607. He was born in Plouguerneau in 1577 and died in Le Conquet

Chapelle de St-Michel

(see page 100) in 1652, where he is also honoured. He was a fervent missionary in the Catholic Reform movement, using painted animal skins or wooden panels (taolennoù) to bring the bible and moral tales alive for a peasant audience. Examples can be seen when the oratory is open in summer.

The commemorative cross in the pine trees (on private property) nearby is for the steamer Kurdistan, wrecked a long way from here, near the Scilly Iles, but with some bodies (perhaps from a lifeboat trying to reach shore) arriving here in 1910.

Rochers de St Michel Another work by local sculptor François Breton can be seen just off the path.

Rochers de St-Michel

In the vicinity

Plouguerneau This attractive little *bourg* is worth visiting, especially for the excellent *Musée des Goémoniers et de l'Algue*, all about the fascinating history of seaweed gathering and usage.

No.19 TRÉMAZAN   Circular   Grade 1   12km

This is given as a circular walk, but the unspoilt coastline section with its sensational rock formations and exquisite cliff-top chapel would also provide a satisfying out and back route.
The walk begins by crossing the interior via quiet roads and a long stretch on a former railway line before reaching the coast at Kersaint near the beach and ruined castle of Trémazan. From there an increasingly beautiful path follows this rock-strewn littoral to the exceptional Pointe de Landunvez.
Note the wayside crosses, a characteristic of the Pays d'Iroise area.

Starting point: the parking lay-by on the D127 coastal road at Kerlaguen (see map).

Kersaint The chapel (15th century) is dedicated to Ste Haude (or Aude), who in legend was decapitated by her brother Gourguy after their step-mother's lies convinced the young man that his sister was unchaste. A stained glass window tells her story. Haude appeared at the château carrying her own head and denounced her step-mother, who was struck down on the spot. In remorse Gourguy devoted himself to God and was later known as Saint Tanguy.

The building dates from the 15th century with later restorations. There is an unusual ossuary structure with places for skulls opposite the west door.

Wayside cross

The **Maison des Chanoines** (16th century) housed the priests who officiated in the chapel, canons in the service of the Du Chastel family, who owned the nearby castle of Trémazan.

Château de Trémazan This romantic medieval ruin dates back probably to the 11th century although with much later development. It was the property of the powerful Du Chastel family for hundreds of years, before being abandoned in the 18th century. Part of the tower fell in 1995, revealing the internal structure of the square keep.

Château de Trémazan

Directions

A *Detour to La Maison des Chanoines: look for narrow passage on left, beside a garage, emerging in Route des Chanoines next to the 16th century house. Then return.*

B *a) Detour left along Impasse du vieux Château to get a glimpse of the ruined keep and the dovecote, then return.*
b) From this crossroads a footpath shadows the road ahead nearer to the coast and terminates in a parking lay-by at Trémazan.

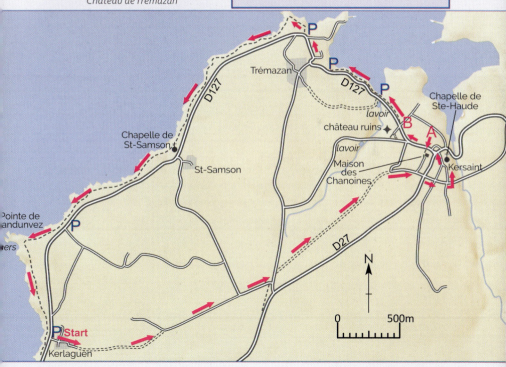

Trémazan

Chapelle de St-Samson

Fontaine and cross below the Chapelle de St-Samson

The simplicity of this little chapel, unusually placed right on the cliff, is a reflection of the openness and wild nature of the landscape around this coast. This version dates from 1785, but the spot has been a site of worship since Neolithic times.

St Samson was one of the seven founding saints of Brittany, arriving from Wales in the 6th century and finally becoming bishop of Dol-de-Bretagne. The waters of the *fontaine* below the chapel near the rocks were said to cure rheumatism and eye problems. Beside this stands a fine monolithic granite cross.

Pointe de Landunvez Above the point, a red and white daymark beside ruined buildings of the former semaphore station, destroyed by the Germans before Liberation in WWII, is an important navigational reference point and very visible on this low coast. The granite rock formations above the sea are of massive form, rounded and striated into memorably tortuous shapes.

Pointe de Landunvez

No.20 POINTE de DOUBIDY — Circular — Grade 2 — 9km

This is a very quiet route with many spectacular views in different directions over the Rade de Brest. As the coastal path does not cover this peninsula and there is no road access to the Pointe de Doubidy, it is much less well-known and well-walked than the many other promontories onto the inland sea. The route is mainly easy-going on tracks, mostly level in the first part of the walk, but a little more challenging in a few places when crossing back over the peninsula. Some areas may be wet in all seasons.

Starting point: the chapel of St-Guenolé on the south side of the Anse de Lauberlac'h, five kms from the *bourg* of Plougastel. Follow Tinduff, then chapel signs (see map).

The chapel of St-Guenolé dates from the 16th century, with a transept added in the 17th. The *calvaire* bears the date 1654. Land here was originally given to the monks of Landévennec Abbey, who honoured their founder St Guenolé with a shrine.

Table of orientation From here the military port of Le Fret is visible to the west, and in the distance to the south the distinctive heights of Menez Hom. Just opposite to the north is the little harbour of Lauberlac'h. The peninsula where it stands obscures the sight of Brest.

Anse de l'Auberlac'h

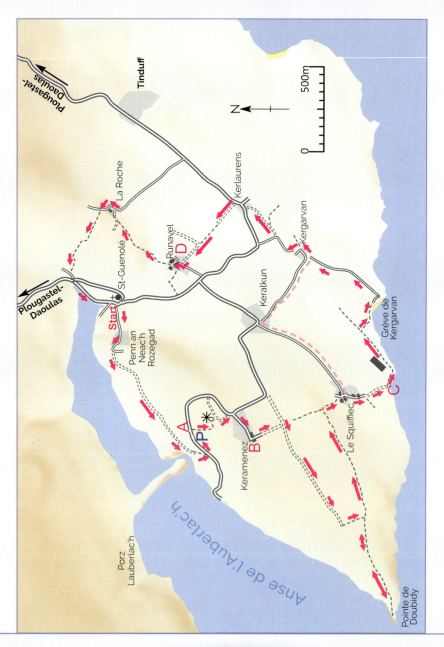

Pointe de Doubidy

Rade de Brest from Pointe de Doubidy

Pointe de Doubidy & Rade de Brest It is well worth a diversion out to the point. From the top there are panoramic views of the Rade de Brest, with the île Ronde ahead. This inland sea of more than 150km², separated from the Atlantic by a narrow channel (Le Goulet) has provided Brest with an exceptional protected harbour. This has been a major site of the French navy since the 17th century, and an important German submarine base during WWII.

A little path leads downhill right to the rocks on the point. On the way there is a tiny circle of grass and rocks to sit on making a good spot for a picnic or pause.

La Roche In this hamlet, the route turns left immediately after the oldest house in the commune of Plougastel, with its fine stone framed windows. The date reads 1589.

DIRECTIONS

A At end of large parking area on right, turn right up narrow footpath. Follow up to Table of Orientation.

B Turn left on very narrow road between houses.

C From this pebbly beach the route leads along the top of fields to a larger one, the Greve de Kergarvan. At the highest tide it may not be possible to cross the beaches: in which case, follow the alternative route on the map from Le Squiffiec via Keralkun to Kergarvan.

D At the end of the track turn right on road in Runavel, bear left between two little stone houses, continue 40m to sharp left bend and footpath is on right between houses.

Alternatively, continue to end of the road and another footpath on right to return directly to St-Guenolé by the road.

No.21 MENEZ DREGAN Circular   Grade 1   7.2km

This easy walk combines a pretty river valley containing examples of industrial and religious heritage with a sensational stretch of coastline, famous for its archaeological remains. The route starts in the little harbour of Pors Poulhan, maritime outpost of Pays Bigouden.

Starting point: Pors Poulhan, large carpark opposite the port area (see map).

Pors Poulhan Just beyond the car-park to the south, a statue of a woman in traditional dress of Pays Bigouden stands on the coast. Her presence marks the boundary of this region which extends south to Penmarc'h and its 'capital', the town of Pont l'Abbé. A story claims that the distinctive tall headdress or *coiffe* commemorates the church towers truncated in revenge for local uprisings in the revolt of 1675.

Moulin(s) de Tréouzien This recently restored water-mill in a verdant valley was built in 1812 and abandoned in the mid 20th century. It is now open to the public and produces bread for sale at weekends. On the other side of the path on a rise stands the base of a former windmill, also due for restoration. Both mills once belonged to a local manor house.

Moulin de Tréouzien

Chapelle de St-They The path passes a large *lavoir* before the slope leading up to the isolated setting of the plain little chapel of St-They (St Day in Cornwall) and its *fontaine*, dating from the 17th century with later restoration. The waters of the spring were said to cure rheumatism. St They was a disciple of the great St Guenolé: a window in the chapel has scenes from his life.

Seaweed oven Beside the path is a seaweed oven, remnant of a vital industry on this coastline. After being gathered from the shore or seabed, the seaweed was dried in stacks (see p.98), then burnt in ovens like this one. This produced blocks of sodium carbonate or *'pain de soude'*, which was taken to factories by cart. Seaweed was used in the manufacture of glass, paper and soap. Another important product was iodine: it took five to six tons of seaweed to produce about 2- 3kg of iodine.

Directions

A *A brief diversion here leads to an old windmill tower.*
B *It is possible to cut straight across to the coast here by turning left.*
C *A very narrow path descends through the gorse and heather.*

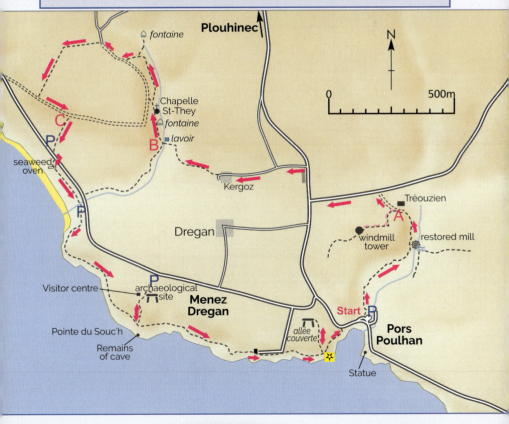

Menez Dregan

Menez Dregan & Pointe du Souc'h The coastal path skirts the cliff-side remains of an important paleolithic site. A cave (now collapsed and covered with metal sheets for protection) provided archaeologists with evidence of the use of fire by man 450,000 years ago. The cave was a natural point for shelter and observation of the surroundings, and researchers have been able to distinguish six levels of human occupation at different times. No actual human remains were found - the soil is very acidic - but the tooth of an elephant survived.

On the headland above is a major Neolithic necropolis with numerous burial places once covered by a great cairn, now partly restored. There were several phases of construction over the two

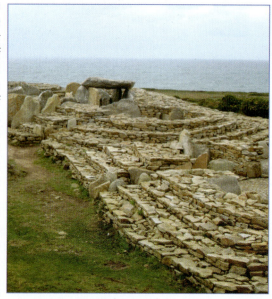

Partly restored cairn

thousand years following c4500BC. One large chamber contained an individual burial together with a polished axe, arrowheads, flint, a round-bottomed vase and a pottery bottle - presumably containing the essentials of food and drink for the symbolic journey from life to death. Other dolmens contained collective burials, perhaps of family groups.

The interpretation centre, with artefacts and visual aids to understand the development of the site, also has a roof-top viewing platform. Before the slope down to the cliff, there is a special shelter where reconstruction drawings viewed against the current seascape show how the landscape has changed since pre-historic times - surprisingly little, apart from the rise in sea levels which has covered the plain where mammoth and rhinoceros once roamed. A series of well-illustrated panels ranged over the site offers a detailed interpretation of visual remains.

Allée couverte at Pors Poulhan It's worth a slight detour to see this huge Neolithic burial place. In the form of an *allée couverte*, or covered alleyway, although only two of the 3 or 4 original massive cap-stones remain, it measures 10.8m long and up to 2m wide. Partly destroyed by the Germans in WWII, it remains an impressive monument. The Chévalier de Fréminville, an enthusiastic antiquarian writing about 1835, described this as the largest and most beautiful dolmen in Finistère. Excavation in the 1980s yielded finds from Neolithic pottery to Gallo-Romano funerary urns.

Allée couverte

No.22 PENMARC'H   Circular   Grade 1   12.4km

The impressive section of coastline on the South-west tip of Finistère, marked by a famous lighthouse, offers a level walk which combines exceptional natural scenery and many sights of interest. Near the start point at Plage Pors Carn, which has a panoramic view of the Baie d'Audierne, is the Pointe de la Torche, a famous surfing venue, with a Neolithic dolmen and WWII German bunker cheek by jowl on the rocky headland.

Starting point: Pors Carn beach, the parking area opposite the Museum of Prehistory (see map).

The Museum of Prehistory This museum was founded in 1924 with the idea of bringing together artefacts from archaeological digs all over Finistère. Today, thousands of objects represent history from the Paleolithic to medieval periods. The display includes a reconstruction of the necropolis from nearby St-Urnel, a remarkable Dark Age burial ground with remains from about AD500. Many reconstructed exhibits can be seen in the grounds outside at any time.

Seaweed oven The collection and processing of seaweed was an important local industry (see p.79 & 97 for details).

Les Rochers The '*rokkes blake*' (black rocks) of Saint Guenolé were a key element of the story in Chaucer's 14th century Franklin's Tale, as Dorigen feared for her husband's safe return from a journey to England. At low tide it is easy to see how treacherous the flat ranks of rocks are for sailors, but there is also danger for those on the land. In 1870, the family of the Prefect of Finistère were picnicking on the higher rocks here when a freak wave swept them away. An iron cross flat in the rocks (where the railing is today) marks the spot. It is still a place of fatal accidents and care is essential.

Seaweed oven

Océane Alimentaire This large outlet for local products also contains a very detailed visual display about the history of the area and is well worth a visit.

Chapelle de Notre-Dame de la Joie One of the few built directly on the sea front in Brittany, this late 15th century chapel with its maritime motifs and votives in thanks for survival at sea reflects faith in the face of danger. In floods of 1896 it was filled with seaweed and pebbles, but remained structurally sound.

Lighthouses The earliest warning system for sailors here was a fire tower on the little 15th century chapel of St-Pierre, patron of the harbour. The first lighthouse, built in 1835, is now a marine exhibition centre. The magnificent Phare Eckmühl (1897) was financed by an inheritance from the daughter of Nicolas Davout, whom Napoleon appointed Prince of Eckmühl after a victorious battle there. It is 66m high and has a range of 44km. Open to the public at certain times.

Phare Eckmühl

Lifeboat Papa Poydenot A restored lifeboat from the era of rescue by sail and oar-powered vessels can be visited in the boat-shed by the old lighthouse. There is also an impressive display of photos and written accounts demonstrating the heroism and tragedy of lifeboat history on this dangerous shore.

Église Ste-Thumette, Kerity

Kerity - port, church and houses Kerity's past prosperity as an important port can be seen by some fine old stone houses surviving in the village, once homes of wealthy ship-owners. The church of Ste Thumette has undergone many changes over the centuries, with a porch dating from the 15th. One account of 1835 claims it once belonged to the Knights Templar. In ruins at the end of the 19th century, it has since been partly restored.

The walled Manoir de Kerousy with its impressive entrance gate and dovecote dates from the 15th century. A cat-slide roof and square stair-tower can be seen at the rear.

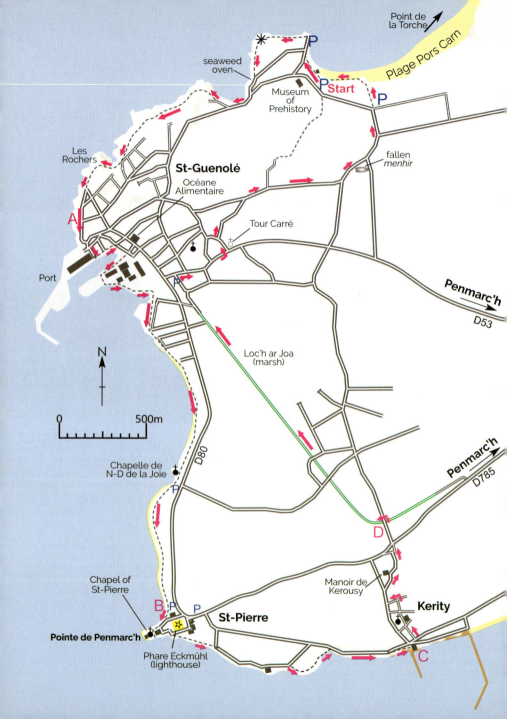

Phare Eckmühl and Chapelle N-D de la Joie from the old railway line across the marsh Loch ar Joa

Train Birinik This short railway line of 17.8km opened in 1907, linking the coast here with the markets of Pont l'Abbé, the main town of Pays Bigouden. A slow train nicknamed *train birinik* (limpet) carried fish, potatoes and tourists until 1963.

Tour Carrée This tower (1488) is all that remains of the former parish church of St-Guenolé. It was abandoned in the mid 18th century, but some improvements were made later, like a roof for the tower in 1845. Carvings of ships (and fish) on the monumental west porch reflect the economy of the area.

DIRECTIONS

A *Follow high level walkway along sea wall. At end rejoin road and turn right, then go ahead into port area. Turn left along quay, then right across end of harbour and right again into opposite port area. Care needed, these are working areas.*

B *Keep to seaward side of carpark and continue on footpath between low stone walls. At road bear right towards the point. Allow time to explore this interesting area.*

C *Go right up to harbour building and cross road immediately after mini-roundabout on long crossing, bear right (rue Victor Hugo) and then left immediately up a narrow lane (Hent Fitur Koz).*

D *Turn left onto former railway track, now a cycle route.*

No.23 DOËLAN Circular Grade 1 5.2km

This is a short, easy walk combining the most picturesque of little ports with a stretch of wild coastline and a cross-country return with sea views - just the thing for working off a good lunch in one of the various water-side restaurants.

Starting point: the waterfront at Doëlan Rive Gauche. Turn left before the lighthouse to carpark on left (see map).

Doëlan The port is famous for its pair of small striped lighthouses, red and white on the right bank of estuary and green and white by the harbour. For much of its history, it has been a centre of sardine and mackerel fishing, although today the pleasure-boat anchorage is just as important to the local economy.

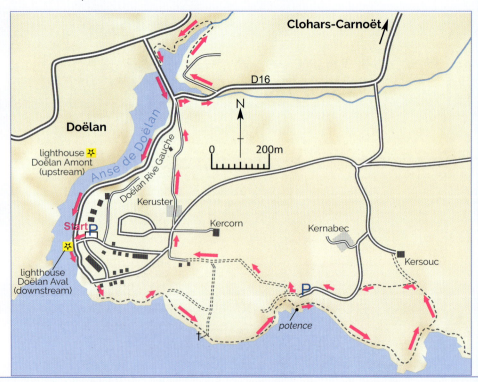

Red lighthouse (aval) on the other side of the creek

Port Blanc The simple and very moving granite *calvaire* with its elongated figures on the point is by Breton sculptor André Boureau, and dates from 1971.

Seaweed industry Once an important source of revenue in this area, the seaweed industry has left its mark here with a remaining *potence*, a post used for hauling up baskets of seaweed from the rocks, and stone-walling to secure the cliff faces. There has been strong local opposition to a recent proposal to exploit this area for *algues* once again on a large scale using modern machinery.

Calvaire by André Boureau

The return journey through **Keruster** passes village houses, including a very fine example of local thatch, and the narrow streets typical of a port exposed to strong winds, before an optional extension around the creek on a narrow path to return to the starting point.

> Because of its charm and archetypal Breton coastal atmosphere, episodes of the French version of TV series Doc Martin have been filmed here, with Doëlan becoming 'Port Garrec' for the purposes of fiction.

No.24 MENEHAM   Linear   Grade 1   8km one way

This is the top spot on the north coast for an easy stroll by the sea, with something for all the family. Walk out for half an hour in either direction from the parking area by massive rock formations that hide a little look-out post used from the mid 18th century by coastguards and customs officers watching for smugglers on the Channel. To the east is a beautiful sandy beach for swimming or just lazing about. It is only 3.6km to the famous Men Marz menhir.

There is considerable historic interest here too. By the rocks are drying seaweed stacks and a seaweed oven sunken into the ground and still used today for demonstrations of an industry that was formerly a crucial part of the local economy.

Just behind is the 19th century village of Meneham, which grew up on the site where the soldiers had been garrisoned, with peasants struggling to make ends meet by fishing and collecting seaweed. It has now been restored with traditional methods and local materials (such as thatch), and contains exhibitions, artisans' outlets, an *auberge* for refreshments, accommodation for walkers and the village bread-oven, used as part of the many festivities organized in season to preserve the memory of this traditional community..

Seaweed stacked ready for burning

Look-out post

This part of the Finistère coast has long been known as the **Pays pagan**, a dangerous area for shipping, where tales of wrecking and smuggling reflected the supposedly outlandish character of the inhabitants.

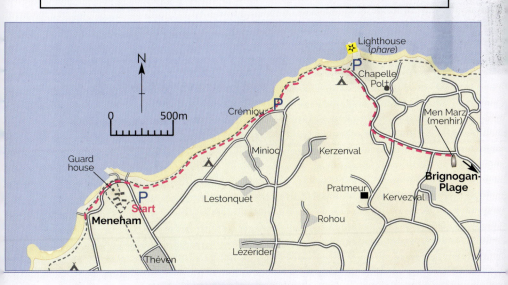

No.25 LE CONQUER to FORT DE BERTHAUME
Linear Grade 2 12.5km one way

This stretch of coast offers serious historical interest with the old *bourg* in Le Conquet, a ruined cliff-top abbey at the Pointe St-Mathieu and an island fort on the approach to Plougonvelin. Cliffs pierced by deep caves, rocky fingers sneaking out from below the water and the splendid sea views towards the archipelago of Molène, formerly part of the European land mass, and the Crozon peninsula to the south all add up to an exceptional walk in either or both directions. The route is generally easy going, without extreme ups and downs, but there are plenty of undulations and steps to negotiate along the way..

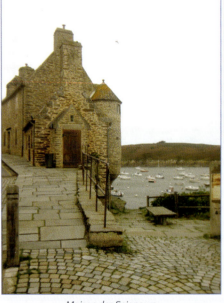

Maison des Seigneurs

Starting point: the old port of **Le Conquet**, with its strong fishing traditions and ancient houses, like the Maison des Seigneurs (1510) on the estuary (see map). It is also gateway to the Atlantic islands with daily boats to Molène and Ouessant.

From above the port, the coastal path takes the road to the **Pointe de Renards** where a footpath soon leads to a little round concrete **look-out tower**. Beyond here the route snakes along below the main road, occasionally touching it briefly, and the lighthouse on the point ahead can soon be seen in the distance. In the car-park at **Porz Liogan** is a granite memorial stele for five RAF pilots shot down in July 1943.

Pointe St-Mathieu is a dramatic location at the mouth of the Rade de Brest, an important strategic setting to protect the WWII German submarine base in Brest. Today it contains a curious mixture of historical memories. In an old fort at sunken level is a **WWI memorial** for sailors lost during the war, fronted

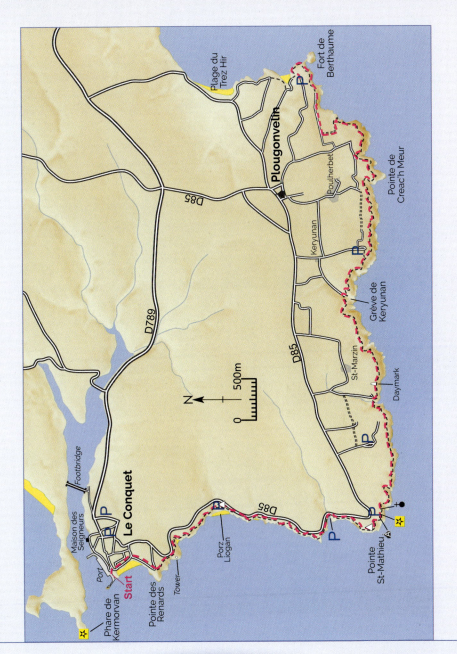

Le Conquet to Fort de Berthaume page 101

WWI memorial

by a huge column (1927) topped by the head of a grieving Breton widow by sculptor Réné Quillivic. The artillery battery beside it dates from the 18th century and was later re-used: the guns on display date from 1888. Dominating the skyline behind is **the lighthouse** (1835), a signalling station (1906 with modernizations) and the imposing ruins of a **Benedictine abbey**, accompanied by a 19th century chapel with a 14th century doorway from an earlier building. The legendary foundation of the abbey was by St-Tanguy in the 6th century, housing the relics of the Apostle Saint Matthew brought from Egypt by Breton sailors. Romanesque remains can be seen today, including the stunted base of a fire-tower the monks used to warn shipping of the cliffs.

After the point, the route is rarely anywhere near a road and offers that exhilarating sense of being alone in the world with only the waves and the gulls for company. WWII fortifications become more and more apparent, part of the Atlantic Wall of German defences. Today most are scrawled with often artistic grafitti, like the huge concrete structure with a striking 'peaked cap'

Pointe St-Mathieu

right beside the path. Remnants of typical coastal activity can be seen in the holed and notched stones on the cliff-edge, used for hauling up valuable driftwood or seaweed for industrial processing. Walls reinforce the cliffs for safety at such working points.

One of the beauties of this path is the **view ahead** to the Crozon peninsula, particularly the Pointe de Pen Hir and Les Tas de Pois (piles of peas, describing the series of off-shore rocks) near Camaret, and beyond that Cap Sizun, culminating in the Pointe du Van. There is some variety of path, from open sections alongside fields and beside a gleaming white daymark (navigational aid) to broad tracks between gorse hedges cutting off the sea, and steep steps around sunken lakes and down to the scarily rocky mooring for boats at the Grève de Keryunan.

Sight of the **Fort de Berthaume** is obscured almost to the last minute by a jutting headland around the Pointe de Creac'h Meur, but the revelation is worth the wait. Because of cliff erosion, the final approach detours inland via a little road and then a footpath to pass very close to the island fort and all its defence mechanisms. Louis XIV's chief engineer Vauban saw the potential of this site and established a fort here in 1689. A 'flying boat' or winch with cradle was used for the crossing, although the rock is accessible at low tide. Its guns worked in tandem with those at Camaret across the water to foil a Dutch-English attack in 1694. The current remains, from a later date including WWII when it was used by the German occupying forces, can be visited at certain times.

Fort de Berthaume

Return by bus An alternative to returning all the way on foot to Le Conquet, is to take the line 11 bus back there from Plougonvelin (or to Brest in other direction). After the fort, continue on the coast path all the way to the Plage de Trez Hir, a large beach. There's a bus-stop on the road just here. Check times in advance on the website **via0029.fr**

No.26 LANDÉVENNEC   Linear   Grade 2   8km one way

This glorious wooded linear route beside the broad Aulne estuary has two focal points and hence two options for either a short, easy out and back to the creek of Moulin Mer (3.5km each way, or an extension to the little *bourg* of Landévennec (8km each way) with its two abbeys, one modern, one medieval, and stunning location on the shore where the great river emerges into the Rade de Brest. The starting point is the spectacular new suspension bridge at Térénez.

Starting point: from Le Faou take the D791, direction Crozon, to the parking area on the Crozon side of the Pont de Térénez. From the viewing platform walk down the track, apparently in the wrong direction but at the bottom turn sharp left and follow path under bridge.

Directions

A *Follow path to right up hill behind chapel. Turn sharp left uphill after 50m.*

B *At this large clearing, go straight on for a challenging continuation along the line of the river. The path is eroded in places and the final ascent up a stream valley needs care (see point D). For a much easier route, turn left steeply uphill to Le Crip..*

C *EITHER take the footpath to the right opposite the buildings to descend into the valley and ascend on a narrow very rocky path OR take a longer route keeping to small roads.*

D *The route now heads steeply up the valley to the main road. Follow the path which weaves back and forth over the stream to a point where there is a clear fork. Go right here over the stream and then up the hillside to the trees bordering the main road. Here there is a narrow gap and a ditch to negotiate.*

Pont de Térénez The new cable-stayed concrete bridge, which opened in 2011, curves in a gracious span of nearly 300m. There is a pedestrian walkway right across beside the road it carries (D791). Designed by Charles Lavigne, it was the first in the world of this type to have such a long bend and has already won various prizes, including the World Infrastructure Award in 2013. Nothing remains of the old bridge (1952) except its western end, now transformed into a large viewing platform, and the views of the estuary and new bridge are indeed spectacular. An even earlier bridge (1925) here was destroyed by the Germans in WWII.

Pont de Térénez

Moulin Mer This tidal-powered grain mill was built in the 15th century by the monks of the abbey at Landévennec. Some of the larger buildings that housed the mechanism were destroyed in a fire in 1956. In its heyday the mill was of great economic importance to the area, processing a thousand 100kg sacks of grain each month, supplied from far and wide by cart and boat.

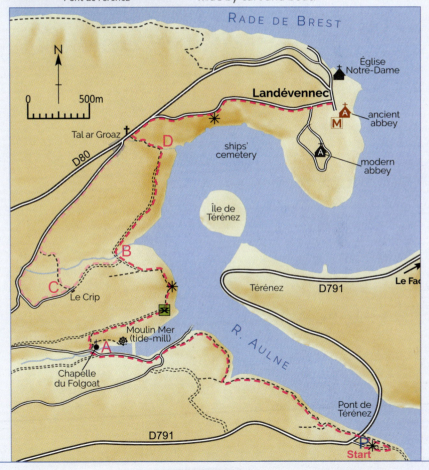

Landévennec

Chapelle de Folgoat (Fool's wood) This pretty little chapel in a forest clearing beside a stream is said to have been the home of a simpleton (fol) or hermit who lived in a tree here during the fourteenth century. He spoke only the words Ave Maria. After his death he was buried here, and an extraordinary lily bearing the same words, sprang up. Investigation revealed that it was sprouting from the mouth of the corpse. This was declared a miracle and a chapel was built on the spot. The actual chapel dates from 1645. It was restored in the 1960s and through the wooden door a stained glass window representing the story can be seen.

Chapelle de Folgoat

Ships' cemetery A viewpoint with seats overlooks the location of a last resting-place for ships where, for example, former anti-aircraft vessels await dismantlement.

L'Abbaye de Landévennec The original abbey of Landévennec was founded by St Guenolé, one of the great Breton saints, c485. Under the Benedictine rule from 818, it became a famed seat of learning. Illuminated manuscripts produced by the monks can be seen in the excellent museum attached to the medieval abbey today. This structure sits on the shore of the estuary, which made it vulnerable to a Viking attack in 913 which destroyed the earliest version. The current extensive ruins are from later reconstructions. Sold into private hands after the Revolution, the site came back into Benedictine ownership in 1950 and a new monastery was built further up the hill. Today this houses a research library, the Bibliothéque bretonne, and has a large shop with books and gifts. Both abbeys can be visited.

Landévennec The attractive village of Landévennec offers limited possibilities for refreshments, depending on the season. Evidence of the local micro-climate can be seen in the presence of palm trees and mimosa adorning the numerous holiday villas. It is worth strolling along to the idyllic setting of the little 17th church of Notre-Dame with its sloping floor and old paintings, including one of St Corentin and the cathedral at Quimper.

No.27 CHÂTEAU DE DINAN to CAP DE LA CHÈVRE

Linear   Grade 3   9.9km one way

This is a section of the most spectacular Brittany coastal walking, with the added bonus of the Crozon peninsula's distinctive geological identity. It would be good to visit the excellent Maison des Mineraux in nearby St-Hernot before or after the walk if possible. Wonders on this route include a raised beach and pillow lavas to be seen on beaches below the coastal path. It also features a stunning natural rock formation, an unusual Iron Age fortified promontory and an elaborate WWII memorial. Because of a lack of habitations and parking areas directly on the coastline, this stretch of littoral is unfrequented outside the main season apart from the two viewpoints at the start and finish.

Starting point: The route starts southwards from the parking area at the Pointe de Dinan, but do begin by going up onto the headland to see the '**Château de Dinan**', the name stemming from the fortress-like impression and rocky arches of this natural formation. Again before picking up the coastal path, go down onto the beach of Porz Koubou to see the geological feature of a raised beach (see map).

Pointe de Dinan to Cap de la Chèvre Starting the walk, a narrow path ripples across the moor and then over the first headland to descend to a pebbly beach at Porz Mel before rising quickly and following the cliffs again through gorse and heather. The lower, grassy promontory of **Lostmarc'h** can be seen protruding ahead, but it is not until coming over the last rise and looking down on the site that the defensive lines of ditches and ramparts come into view.

This well-preserved Iron Age work dates from c500BC and represents an area where the community could shelter in times of attack. This was also an important Neolithic site with small *menhirs* and burial chambers on the hillside. On the beach below (south side of northern point) pillow-lavas thrust up by underwater eruptions c440 million years ago can be seen, a series of 'pillow' shaped rocks cemented by limestone.

Raised beach at Porz Koubou

Cap de la Chèvre

The route continues above the beach, passing between sand-dunes and reedy marshland, although it is possible simply to walk along the sand and then scramble up to rejoin the path above. At the far end are WWII devices, the first sign of many **defensive structures** down this coastline. The path directly passes a couple of bunkers on the next point, and above the Plage de la Palue, large casements overlooking a possible landing point are visible in the side of the cliff.

A series of headlands, including the distinctive Beg ar C'houbez, giving bird's eye views of some astonishing rock forms now follows, with one path usually near the edge of the cliffs and alternatives for short cuts over the shoulder, and inland diversions to cross coves. One section passes through areas of reclaimed land marked out by dry-stone walling, now mostly filled with gorse. The **semaphore station** which monitors marine security on the Cap de la Chèvre soon makes its tantalizing appearance ahead, but there are still two steep ups and downs to negotiate before emerging on the plateau. (Taking evasive action on narrow grassy paths will lead to the parking area behind the semaphore.) On the point itself is a **WWII monument** shaped like a plane's wing to commemorate the heroic actions of naval aviators.

In the vicinity
Maison des Mineraux This fascinating and well-presented exhibition in the village of St-Hernot presents the detail of Crozon's exceptionally rich geology, and also gives a wider perspective of the rocks of the Armorican Massif. Most entertaining is a dark room of glowing fluorescent minerals - a remarkable colour spectacle. **www.maison-des-mineraux.org**

From Beg ar C'houbez

No.28 POINTE du MILLIER to KASTEL KOZ

Linear   Grade 3   9.6km one way

Walking west from this wonderful viewpoint will provide the very best of coastal walking in Brittany, from paths winding gently across rounded heather-topped headlands to steep descents into sandy bays. There are also opportunities for rocky scrambles by exploring a promontory once fortified in the Iron Age. Forays inland can include the idyllic setting of the Moulin de Keriolet with its rocky chaos and the little *bourg* of Beuzec with its magnificent church. The walk offers views of the Crozon peninsula across the Bay of Douarnenez, including the striking Cap de la Chèvre (see pages 107-9).

Starting point: the carpark behind Pointe du Millier. Pointe du Millier is signed from the D7, via the D407.

Start from the inland parking area and either descend steps straight down to the coastal path or (better) walk out (700m) to the actual point, passing the track to see the **Moulin de Keriolet**, with its impressive working wheel, and the chance to visit the interior in season. The setting in a rocky valley is very beautiful and worth the detour. Cross the stream via the stones of a granite chaos to see 'the boat' in which St Conogan is said in legend to have travelled from Britain. It may in reality have been one of a pair of standing-stones in Neolithic times.

Lighthouse, Pointe du Millier

The **Pointe du Millier** has the unusual feature of a lighthouse contained within the structure of a cliff-top house, dating from 1881, with decorative stonework on the landward windows.

From here the coastal path snakes away westwards across the headlands and is easy to follow.

The beach in a deep bay at **Pors Péron** makes a good resting point. The coastal path turns inland up the road for a short distance here before regaining the headland to descend sharply to another cove. This was the scene on the night of August 23rd 1943 for a clandestine embarkation when Joseph Marec, his crew and 14 passengers set sail for England to join the Free French forces. A plaque commemorates the event.

The path then undulates through the heather around the **Pointe de Trénouaret**, behind the rocky edges of this heavily indented coastline. **Kastel Koz** can be seen ahead, jutting out into the ocean. This promontory was fortified by Celtic tribes in the Iron Age, forming a defensive feature known as a *éperon barré*. Natural rocky barriers and manmade bank and ditch earthworks protected people and livestock sheltered on the extremity of the peninsula. Excavations of the site in the 19th century suggested that about 200 people could be installed here. Finds of Iron Age pottery, iron objects and a bronze dagger were made. It is possible to go right out to the striated granite rock formations at the very end here.

Kastel Koz

From this point a path leads uphill off the coastal path to a parking area. From here continue straight ahead on the road to reach the *bourg* of **Beuzec**, which has shops, refreshments and a tourist office. The church of Notre-Dame de la Clarté (formerly of St-Budoc) has elements from the 15-17th century (tower from 1552, a fine porch of 1648), restored after destruction in a fire in 1936.

Pors Lanvers

In the vicinity

Réserve du Cap Sizun A few kilometres further along this northern coast is a nature reserve with viewing platforms for a perspective on the thousands of sea-birds which live, visit and nest here - cormorants, guillemots, choughs and peregrine falcons to name but a few. Access is signed to the right off the D7 before Goulien.

At the end of this peninsula are two spectacular headlands, the **Pointe du Van** and the **Pointe du Raz**, separated by the **Baie des Trépassés**, with its deep beach and dramatic breakers. The Pointe du Van is usually the better option for a quiet stroll, as it is much less frequented than its famous neighbour. There are panoramic views and a focal point in the chapel and *fontaine* of St-They, perched on the cliffside. Despite not quite being the westernmost point of France (this honour being held by the Pointe de Corsen north of Brest), the Pointe du Raz is a veritable tourist honey-pot throughout the year. Moving away from the area around the point itself will soon see an end to the crowds, however, and the coastal path offers good views of the tiny, flat Île de Sein across one of the most turbulent passages of Breton waters.

THE MONTS d'ARRÉE

The highest hills in Brittany offer many options for walkers, taking in the key elements of the landscape: rocky crests, rough tracks over open moorland (*landes*) and peat-bogs (*tourbières*) traversed by wooden walkways. Long views are a big attraction, north to the ferry at Roscoff, west to Menez Hom and south to the Montagnes Noires.

The area remains relatively uncultivated, although some small fields are still cut for hay or carry a seasonal crop of *blé noir* (sarrasin), which thrives in poor soil. Away from the paths immediately surrounding the parking area at the Ferme des Artisans (also called Ferme d'Antea) and Mont St-Michel-de-Brasparts with its landmark little chapel perched on the top, the walking trails are usually very peaceful and it is easy to get a sense of isolation in a wild landscape. The maps should help in creating plenty of other walks. Some of the best available featured in my previous volume Walking in Finistère.

Three hundred million years ago the Monts d'Arrée were part of the same mountain range as the Alps. Their exposed position on the western edge of Europe has made them very vulnerable to erosion and the main crests today are of schist and quartzite rather than granite. 'Mountains no longer, they remember what they were', said Anatole Le Braz (1859-1926), a reference to the remarkable atmosphere of this area unique in Brittany, despite their rather lowly stature. The highest point, Roc'h Ruz, is only 387m. Easily accessible heights include Roc'h Trévézel, Tuchenn Gador and Mont St-Michel de Brasparts.

Moors

The Yeun Elez, a vast bowl of marsh, is crossed by the Elez river, which was used to create a lake and barrage for hydro-electricity in 1930, thus curtailing much of the previous workings of peat for fuel. It is the home of Breton legend and was said to contain the entrance to the Celtic underworld. It is also the location of one of France's earliest nuclear power stations, which has been decommissioned for decades and is in the slow process of dismantlement. The wetlands now harbour a colony of beavers at the Tourbière du Venec and the distinctive flora can be examined at close quarters on the Korrigan Trail at Mougau Bihan near Commana.

The thin acidic soil and harsh weather conditions of this sparsely populated area have contributed to its image as a wild and barren land, a by-word for poverty and hardship in Breton history. The Monts d'Arrée are today part of the regional Parc d'Armorique and contain many small worthwhile exhibitions - like the Wolf Museum at Le Cloître St-Thégonnec, the Maison Cornec at St-Rivoal and the Maison du Recteur at Loqueffret - explaining the unusual development and heritage of the area.

Yeun Elez and Lac St-Michel

WALKING OPTIONS

There are myriad possibilities for enjoying the Monts d'Arrée on foot. This feature contains maps showing various recommended circuits and enough paths for walkers to create their own routes. Four walks giving the varied flavour of the area are shown in more detail, with points of interest described and directional help where necessary.

For those seeking just a very brief taste of this distinctive terrain in the central area around Mont St-Michel-de-Brasparts, two short walks (about 45 minutes each) with great views are marked in blue on the main map. They start from the parking at the Ferme des Artisans, and could be combined for a longer outing.

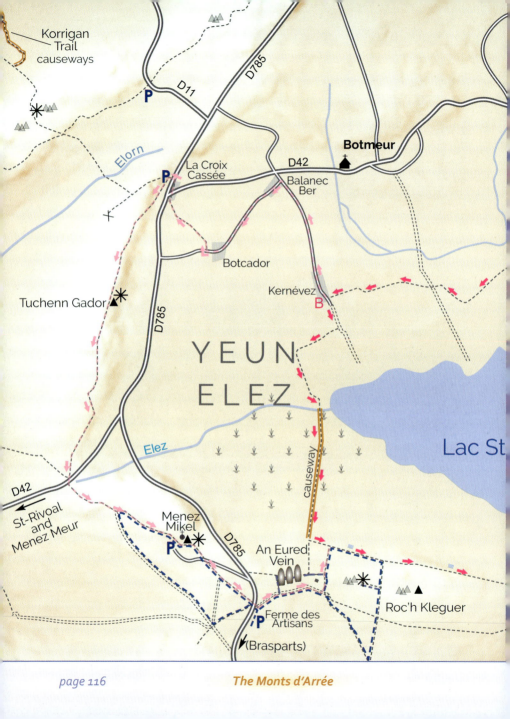

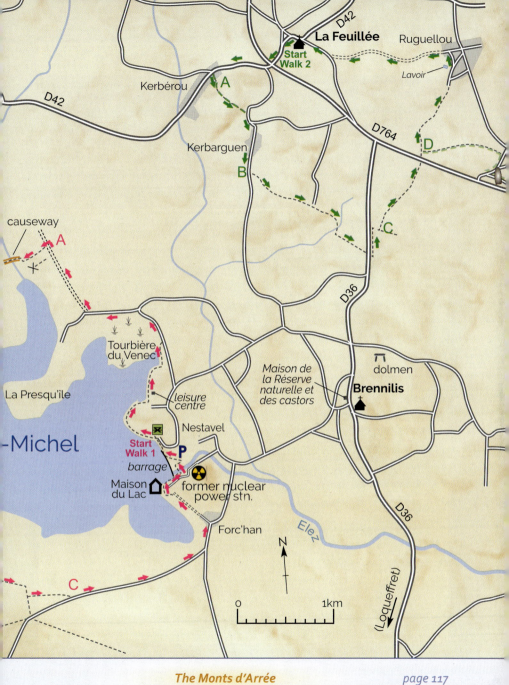

Walk 1 LAC ST-MICHEL AND THE YEUN ELEZ
Circular Grade 1 15km

This fairly flat circumnavigation of the lake has superb views throughout of the moors and peaks, as well as crossing the marshes of the Yeun Elez, on walkways where necessary. It sums up the wild nature of the Monts d'Arrée, despite the presence of a nuclear power station and hydro-electric installations.

Starting point: lakeside picnic area at Nestavel, accessible from the D36 near Brennilis (see map).

DIRECTIONS (see map on p. 116/7)

A *Turn left here - the second of the two paths to the left, 100m apart.*

B *For a longer and more strenuous walk, divert right here to follow a circuit up onto Tuchenn Gador and Mont St-Michel de Brasparts before passing the Neolithic alignment mentioned below to rejoin the lake route. This will add 8 km.*

C *There is no continuous lake path here, although fishermen have created many short stretches of access. It is necessary to follow the road to Forc'han and then resume a footpath to the Maison du Lac.*

Nestavel The lake of St-Michel was created in the early 1930s with a barrage here to generate hydro-electricity. There is also a little beach, picnic tables and a well-laid path beside the lake. Mont St-Michel-de-Brasparts dominates the distant view.

Lac St-Michel from Nestavel

Leisure Centre From the pontoon here there are great views to the northern hills of the Monts d'Arrée. To the right of the communications mast is Roc'h Ruz, a little bump that is actually the highest point in Brittany.

Tourbière du Venec This is where a colony of beavers was introduced in 1968. More about these can be discovered in the *Maison de la Réserve naturelle et des castors* (beavers) in the centre of the village of Brennilis.

Tourbière

Maison du Lac This centre run by the electrical company EDF is open to the public at certain times with displays and information about the nuclear power station, the electricity plant and the lake.

An Eured Vein A short detour here leads to the Neolithic alignment given the name The Stone Wedding Party. According to legend the stones represent revellers turned to stone by the curse of a priest, after they refused to make way for him as he carried the sacrament across the moors to a dying parishioner. Actually the 77 small stones in a wavy line date from about 3000BC and were carefully placed on this plain, open to the sky and with views of Mont St-Michel-de-Brasparts and the other hills, for ceremonial purposes and/or religious rites.

Nuclear power station This was constructed in the early 1960s, one of the earliest in France, in an area chosen for its low population and exploitation. Soon after the area became part of the natural regional Parc d'Armorique for similar reasons! The power station was decommissioned in 1985 with dismantling beginning twelve years later. Since then work has stopped and started according to political will and environmental/safety concerns for workers.

Walk 2 LA FEUILLÉE   Circular   Grade 2   8.2km

This walk starts in a typical Monts d'Arrée village with an interesting history and some attractive old houses in local stone before covering the surrounding countryside on a variety of paths, including a beautiful sunken way, with occasional views to the high hills.

Starting point: centre of La Feuillée, park in central square near the church (see map on p.117).

DIRECTIONS (see map on p.117
A Turn off the road uphill behind a house (sign-post). As the path mounts there are views behind to the crests of the Monts d'Arrée.
B Past the hamlet of Kerbarguen, turn left up a country track.
C Turn (second) left up marked track.
D Take a 1km diversion right here to see the Menhir de Kerelcun.

La Feuillée This is the highest village in Brittany, much changed since it was described in 1794 by Jacques Cambry as a 'poor, abandoned, isolated commune' with infertile land that could not support the population. For this reason many turned to the activity of *pilhaouer* or rag-and-bone man, eeking out a meagre living from this harsh and itinerant lifestyle. From the 15th to 17th century, the Knights of St-John had a major base here and many land-holdings under the *quévaise* system (see p.124). Behind the church an ancient house with a cobbled forecourt is known as the Maison du Commandeur. The striking *auberge* just off the central square is a fine example of a typical 17th century house of this area, with an extended gable and exterior staircase. There is a local form of granite, which was used for the basins of the Fontaine de St-Jean-Baptiste.

The hamlet of Ruguello has a pretty *lavoir* with picnic table nearby.

La Feuillée

The Monts d'Arrée

Walk 3 A WALK ALONG THE CRESTS
Linear　　　　　　　　　Grade 2　　　　　　　　　15km

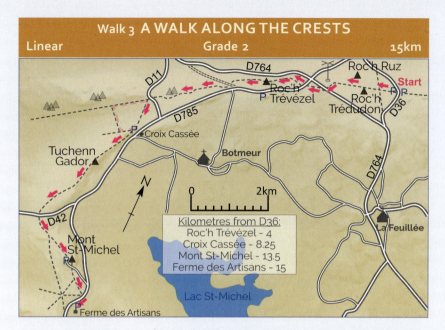

A linear walk along the crests from **Roc'h Trédudon** to **Mont St-Michel-de-Brasparts** will offer superb views to north and south, as well as a new perspective on the expanse of the Yeun Elez. The route passes close to **Roc'h Ruz**, the highest point in Brittany, before skirting the huge communications mast which dominates the ridge. This site - used by French TV - was bombed by Breton nationalists in 1974, and one of the two masts existing then was destroyed.

After crossing the two main roads, the path continues towards **Roc'h Trévezel**, a magnificent outcrop, which towers above the land to the north. This was thought to be the highest point until accurate measurements were made in 2007. There are exceptional views from the top of the rocks.

On reaching the D11, it is possible to cut across to the parking at the foot of Tuchenn Gador by a very narrow and sometimes ill-defined path, or continue ahead and turn down left after 1.2km into the valley where the river Elorn rises, and then up towards the former quarry sites on the north face of the hill ahead. **Tuchenn Gador** ('mound of the chair' (or throne) in Breton) is topped by a natural rock formation of distinctive shape, heavily laced with quartzite. Continue over the summit and down to the D42 for the last stage up to the chapel (1677) at **Mont-St-Michel-de-Brasparts**.

The Monts d'Arrée

Walk 4 MOUGAU BIHAN   Circular   Grade 3   13km

A fine walk involving all the landscape elements typical of the Monts d'Arrée and great views, plus a beautiful lake and an exceptional Neolithic monument. Several variations to cut down on the distance are possible, or it can easily be extended by a 7km circuit of Lac du Drennec.

Starting point: parking for the *allée couverte* at Mougau Bihan, just south of the D764 near Commana (see map).

Directions

A Where the Korrigan trail comes out on a wider track, turn left uphill. At a crossroads of paths, take the narrow one straight ahead to climb to the summit.

B A quick route back to the start point is available here and clearly signed. Another time-saver is to continue straight down hill from Croas Melar and pick up the second half of the circuit.

C Turn sharp left down the side of animal enclosure on very narrow path to descend steeply to the beautiful shady Elorn valley. To avoid this, continue downhill on same path. The two rejoin later.

D On reaching the lake, turn right to continue the 13km walk. If you want to add the circuit of the lake (giving a total of 20km), turn left, and eventually rejoin the original route at the sailing centre.

E At a T-junction of paths, go left and then left again at the next junction.

F At the road go right, back to the car-park at Mougau Bihan.

Mougau Bihan allée couverte

Mougau Bihan
Start
KORRIGAN TRAIL
Quévaise field
A
P
F
B
Croas Melar
E
Kernaman
Kermabil
C
Kerfornédic
Elorn
Kerret
Sailing school
Café
D
Lac du Drennec
Le Drennec
Barrage
N
0 500m

Mougau Bihan - *Allée couverte* This magnificent late neolithic burial site probably dates from 3000-2500BC. It consists of large granite stones forming a long chamber (10m) and a separate *cella* on the southern end, with the entrance to the north. Inside, carvings are still visible: a hafted axe on the stone that divides off the *cella*, and several oar-like images and two pairs of raised bumps, allegedly representing the breasts of a goddess... The capstones were once removed to make a road when the monument was in private ownership.

Korrigan trail This nature trail on wooden walkways examines the flora of the *tourbières*, with information boards in French. The carnivorous *drosera* plant grows near the stream, and the sphagnum moss which characterizes this type of wetland is prolific here.

The *Quévaise* This small oval field (see map) is one of many left-overs from the medieval *quévaise* system, used first by the Cistercian monks of the Abbaye du Relec and later by the Knights of St-John from La Feuillée. To encourage settlers who would clear and work the poor soil, a fairly independent life based on a small house, outbuildings and a piece of land which could be worked in a day (a demi-hectare, as here) was offered.

Korrigan Trail

Views On reaching the path along the ridge, Lac St-Michel and the nuclear power station can be seen ahead. In the foreground is Tuchenn Gador with its distinctive natural outcrop of rocks on the summit and quarries on the north face. The Elorn river rises in the valley below.

Lac du Drennec

Menez Meur

Circuits suitable for family walking can be found in the western Monts d'Arrée at Menez Meur, a natural reserve managed by the regional Parc d'Armorique. A trail of just over 3km introduces Breton breeds of domestic animals such as pigs, goats, sheep and horses, as well as deer and wild boar. Two other short walks of 2.5km each illustrate the characteristics of moorland and forested landscapes. There is also a longer route of 8.5km which gives a wider view, including the craggy peaks so typical of this area. All these walks are well-marked and full of interest.

Follow brown roadsigns to Menez Meur from the D42 at St-Rivoal.

For more details of places to visit in the Monts d'Arrée, see *Things to see and do in the Monts d'Arrée* (reddogbooks.com).

Tro Menez Are

The name means a journey around the Monts d'Arrée. This is an annual day of walks based in a different part of the Monts d'Arrée each May. Circuits of various lengths are available for a small entrance fee, and thousands of people participate in the event. www.tromenezare.bzh

THE NANTES-BREST CANAL

The canal runs right across Brittany, covering a distance of 81kms in Finistère from the Pont de Goariva to Guily Glas near Châteaulin. Most of this consists of the wide Hyères and Aulne rivers, giving a scenic winding course rather than narrow artificial channels. It's a beautiful route for walkers. There is a tow-path (*halage*) all the way along, suitable for walking or cycling, and a *contra-halage* (on the opposite bank) has also been developed. This can be used for an out and back walk. For longer hikes it will be necessary to arrange a lift or taxi back, as public transport in the interior will be of little help.

Note that the locks are numbered from east to west (starting from Nantes, so Lock 192 is the first in Finistère). Suggestions for three of the most attractive linear sections and a circular walk including the towpath are given in this feature. (For the full 365km long-distance walk, see my Nantes-Brest Canal guide.)

The ambitious project of cutting a canal across Brittany was originally given the go-ahead by Napoléon, for a secure land route between the naval bases of Nantes, Lorient and Brest in the face of British blockades of the Breton coast. Work started at the western end at Port Launay in 1811, but it was the 1830s before the entire length was open. What began with a military purpose turned into an economic venture with goods such as grain, wood, sand, stone and coal transported by barge. The heyday was in the late 19th century and early 20th, before the railways and later lorries became clear winners in terms of speed and cost.

In 1923 Lac de Guerlédan was created for a hydro-electric barrage by flooding a 12km section of the Blavet valley in central Brittany. 18 locks and their lock-houses were submerged beneath the new lake. This construction split the canal in two, and it remains un-navigable in central Brittany. It is however functional right across Finistère from the Rade de Brest.

Lock-houses to visit

Selected lock-houses in Finistère are open as interpretation centres for different aspects of the canal. Lock 203 Kergoat covers trees and plants, Lock 209 at Pont Triffen has information about the history and construction of the canal, Lock 224 Rosvéguen portrays the life of lock-keepers, and Lock 232 L'Aulne gives details about fauna along the river. There is also a *passe à poisons* for viewing fish under water at Lock 236 Châteaulin.

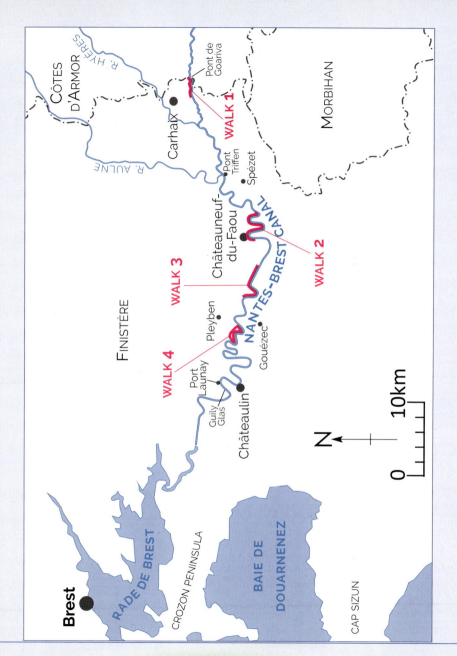

Nantes-Brest Canal

WALK 1 Pont de Goariva to Pont Daoulas
Linear   Grade 1   3.7km one way

This walk gives a good sense of the peaceful atmosphere and lush scenery of the canal in Finistère.

Starting point: the road bridge at Goariva on the D83 Carhaix to Plévin. There is a carpark at the south end of the bridge. The towpath is on the north side of the canal.

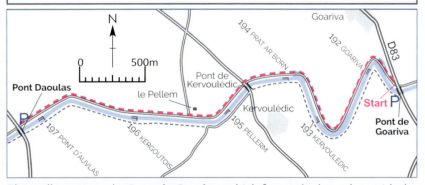

The walk starts at the **Pont de Goariva**, which forms the boundary with the department of Côtes d'Armor to the east. There are six locks in this fairly short stretch, so reserves of water form little lakes to the right of the towpath in places, creating the impression of walking along a causeway. Sharp bends and beautiful mature trees provide constantly changing vistas.

Nantes-Brest Canal

Beyond Lock 195 (Pellem), is the donkey sanctuary *Les anes sont dans le pré* (Donkeys in the meadow), which also offers accommodation (see 'Le Pellem' on map).

There are picnic tables soon after the start and at the end point, as well as seats at intervals along the way. Either return by the towpath or take the *contra halage* for a new point of view and softer conditions underfoot.

On the other side

The *contra halage* offers a return route on the same stretch with a very different perspective. Often the path runs between ranks of trees, an experience lacking on the towpath, and gives the impression of a more secret route. Indeed, very few, except for fishermen, use this great resource. Note that apart from a seasonal cut, this track is little maintained and conditions underfoot can be very wet (long grass) and muddy. In times of flood, the *contra halage* is more vulnerable than the raised towpath, so take special care.

WALK 2 Gwaker to Châteauneuf-du-Faou
Linear — **Grade 1** — **7km one way**

This walk presents the natural beauty and peace that characterise much of the canal in Finistère, but it also offers a view of the economic history of this remarkable waterway, the option of a diversion to a 16th century chapel, and the resources of the pretty town of Châteauneuf-du-Faou.

Starting point: the *passerelle* at Lock 215 (Gwaker or Goaker) where there is plenty of parking. The lock-house is now a *gite d'etape* offering overnight accommodation. Beside the access road is a beautiful centuries-old spreading oak-tree.

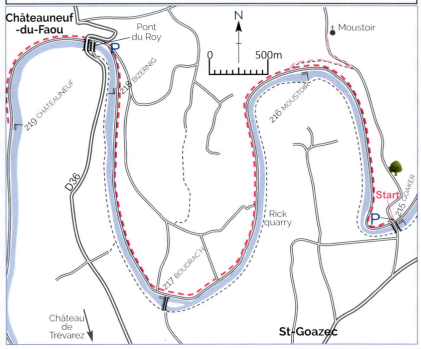

The Aulne Since Pont Triffen, the canal has harnessed the wide and sinuous Aulne river, which will carry it all the way to the end. The deep valley has dense woodland one or both sides for much of the time. There are picnic tables near each of the four locks on this stretch.

Nantes-Brest Canal

Le Moustoir After Lock 216 (Moustoir) a footpath leaves the towpath for a steep climb to the Chapelle du Moustoir, an attractive late 16th century structure with a *calvaire* and well-kept gardens. Open in summer and school holidays.

Rick Quarry The evocative spectacle of a vertiginous hill of slate is a strong reminder of the industrial past of the canal. Rick quarry was only one of the enterprises that lined the route along this section of the canal, with slates taken by barge to Port Launay and then shipped on to numerous destinations. The harsh working conditions can be imagined from the geography of the mine's location.

Lock 217 Boudrac'h There is a *passerelle* at the lock here to cross the river on foot. The Château of Trévarez is 2.6km away. A circular walk including this crossing and the canal is given in *Walking and other activities in Finistère*.

Lock 218 Bizernig This is the headquarters of SMATAH, the organization which manages the canal in Finistère.

Typical kilometre stone

Nantes-Brest Canal

Châteauneuf-du-Faou A steep footpath from the end of the road bridge leads up to the town, which has pretty flowery squares, a range of shops and plenty of refreshment options in bars and restaurants.

Visit the parish church of St-Julien for frescoes by Paul Sérusier, one of the Pont Aven group of artists associated with Gauguin. The Chapel of Notre Dame des Portes, dominating the height above the canal, is a 19th century edifice on the site of the original château, with an impressive 15th century doorway preserved nearby.

On the opposite side of the river, boats, kayaks and mountain bikes can be hired at Aulne Loisirs Plaisance, which also has a café in season.

Pont du Roy An early 17th century bridge, adapted for taller boats in the 19th century by the loss of one arch.

Continue the walk to the next lock (219 Châteauneuf) for a most beautiful canal vista and the sight of the Château de Trévarez on the hill ahead across the water. This early 20th century château was a target for allied bombing in WWII as a German headquarters. The large estate is famous for its collection of azaleas, rhododendrons and camellias.

Return by the same route or cross the river on the Pont du Roy to pick up the *contra halage*. This path may be muddy, wet and a bit overgrown in places outside the summer season.

Châteauneuf-du-Faou

WALK 3 Keriégu to Ty Men

Linear   **Grade 1**   **5.3km one way**

The walk begins with a very rural and remote stretch of towpath. After Lock 223 (Menès) and a long gradual bend, the final straight section leads past Lock 224 (Rosvéguen), where there is an exhibition, to Ty Men and the 'canal antique' of Victor, an old barge.
NOTE: returning from Ty Men by the *contra halage* would add several km to the route as the nearest crossing would be well beyond the starting point, at Pont Pol (on the D72). The total distance of this walk would be 15.8km.

Starting point: Keriégu, accessible from the *bourg* of Lennon (see map).

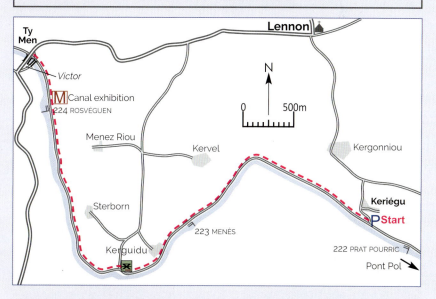

Lock 224 Rosvéguen The exhibition at this lock-house illustrates the life of a lock-keeper when the canal was fully functioning. Artefacts, models, documents and old photographs give a sense of the important practical and social role of the lock-keeper and his family, as well as the hardship of their lives. There is also information about the horses that pulled the barges.

Victor This canal barge or *chaland* was built in Nantes in 1893 and based at Port Launay. It carried fertilizer for farms along the valley and then returned with cargoes of slate collected along the way at Carhaix, Saint Goazec, Châteauneuf and Pont Coblant. This career came to a sad end in 1932 when Victor collided with the bridge at Ty Men in a strong current. It lay lifeless under the bank for 70 years until an association was set up to restore the boat. It now rests by the road over the bridge and can be visited at certain times. Victor is also the focus of an annual fête each September.

'Victor'

Lock-keeper's cottage at Rosvéguen, now an interpretation centre

WALK 4 Pont Coblant   Circular   Grade 2   8.4km

The canal can be seen at its very best on a long stretch of this quiet, verdant walk. A second half on higher ground through farmland offers excellent long views as far as Menez Hom, with the option of then returning beside the canal again or continuing cross-country. Quarries and a lock give the flavour of the Aulne's history here, but it is the natural beauty of a wide and winding river that leaves a lingering impression. The start point of Pont Coblant, with its bar/restaurant and nautical club, is a beautiful spot for relaxing beside the water.

Starting point: Pont Coblant, on the D785 south from Pleyben. Park by the canal (see map).

Quarries After crossing the D785, the route follows the canal towpath for 3.4km. Around the first of many graceful bends, evidence of the former quarrying industry remains to the right, with piles of slate still visible. In the working days of the canal this commodity was taken to Châteaulin by barge and then shipped on around the coast of Brittany. Some went all the way to Paris for building programmes in the French capital.

Overlooking Lock 227 Stéreon

Lock 227 Stéreon The lock-house is now a well-kept private home but the lock itself is used by passing pleasure-craft and the mechanisms for opening and closing the gates can be studied here.

Nantes-Brest Canal

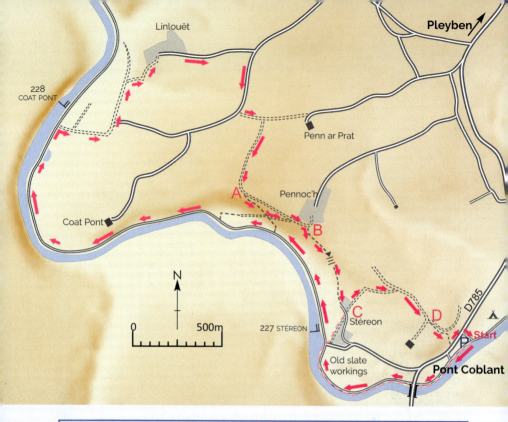

Directions

The route leaves the towpath just before Lock 228 Coat Pont, following a well-made track. A short section of road-walking then leads to a track up over a hill through farmland. **Attention**: access to fields for stock, beware of tape/wire across path, keep dogs on leads.

A *Where the track bends left, take a footpath on the right down into the wood. At a junction of paths turn left uphill to rejoin the higher track.*

B *Before the farm-buildings, take a narrow path off sharp right steeply down the hillside.*

C *On reaching Stéreon EITHER rejoin the towpath and retrace the outward route OR turn left uphill for a cross-country path back to the start.*

D *Where the main track turns right, down to the farm, and another continues ahead, take a narrow path, just to the right of it.*

Stéreon

Châteaulin and Port Launay

The canal flows right through the town at Châteaulin, and three crossing points (a passerelle, a road bridge and a former rail bridge) offer varying perspectives. The *passe à poisons* for viewing fish below the water level is situated near the foot of the latter. A (not very attractive) long road walk beside the water leads to delightful Port Launay with its pleasure boat harbour and a quieter spot to enjoy the canal.

Guily Glas

The name means 'green wood' and the canal ends in this sylvan setting at a last lock (No.237) before the Aulne flows freely to arrive at the Rade de Brest at Landevénnec (see page 104). A recent state-of-the-art barrage at Guily Glas is intended to prevent flooding of the Aulne. The imposing viaduct nearby carries the Quimper/Brest railway.

OUESSANT

The island of Ouessant lies in the Atlantic 20km off the north-west coast of Finistère. It is a rugged and dramatic landscape, measuring approximately 8x4km, providing a coastal walk of nearly 50km which can be easily divided into two, three or four circular routes, depending on the time available for exploration. It is well worth spending three or four days here - the walking is varied and often sensational.

Boats arrive daily from Le Conquet (some starting in Brest) having stopped off first at the small island of Molène, landing at Port du Stiff on the east coast. The only *bourg*, Lampaul, is at the opposite end of the island (4kms away), with a regular, cheap and reliable shuttle bus between the two. Walkers not laden by heavy bags can start walking right from the ferry and take the north or south coast to reach the village.

Because of the absence of provisions outside Lampaul (except a bar/restaurant near the port), it is important to plan supplies in advance and carry plenty of food/water for longer walks. *There is nothing but nature to enjoy around the coastal path*. Don't leave stocking up in Lampaul until the last minute, especially in summer, and it may be necessary to book restaurants in advance in high season. Here it is certainly worth considering hotel package deals with evening meals included, and the option of packed lunches being provided.

Getting to the island: the company Penn ar Bed run ferries to Ouessant with departures from Brest (2hr journey) and Le Conquet (up to 1hr) all year round. The boat makes a stop on the way at the small island of Molène. For details + booking, see **www.pennarbed.fr**

Although there are points of interest in the interior, it is the coast that is so memorable for walkers. Some of the circuit of the island involves high cliffs and careful attention is required, especially in wilder weather. Mostly the walking is easy going with stony or grassy paths (with many variations possible, but it is possible to remain near the coast all the way round) and plenty of opportunities for exploring off-route. Be very careful about swimming - best to stick to sheltered waters between the two western arms, but even here and even in hot weather, the water can be surprisingly chilly.

From spring the upper grasslands and heaths are alive with flowers and in Lampaul itself colours burst rampantly from every garden and window-box. The simple blue and white scheme of the island's houses is a great setting for this powerful display.

> **Beware** The Morganed (male) and Morganezed (female) are legendary beautiful siren people who inhabit their underwater kingdoms and deep caves around the island, and relax on the deserted beaches, combing their long blonde hair. They are a source of unbelievable riches, but sometimes humans pay a heavy price for such favour...

It takes a little imagination to see the land as it was until quite recent times, a patchwork of small walled fields where families grew oats, barley, rye, potatoes and other vegetables, and a proliferation of tiny windmills where they ground their grain. The work was mostly done by woman as the men were away at sea, mainly in the service of the French navy. Remains of star-shaped sheep enclosures designed to offer some protection whatever the weather can still be seen in places. Looking for signs of past usage is one of the subtler interests of walking here.

The island is renowned for its bird life, both resident (50 species nest here) and migratory, as this spot on the extreme tip of Europe is on several over-wintering routes. There are Atlantic puffins on the offshore Île de Keller, and a colony of seals in the area around Ouessant and Molène. The famous black bee of the island, protected by isolation from the sad decline of mainland bee populations, is much prized for its excellent honey.

If you want to enjoy the paths in relative tranquillity, spring and autumn are the best times to visit Ouessant. The only certainty about a winter visit is that there will be some dramatic weather.

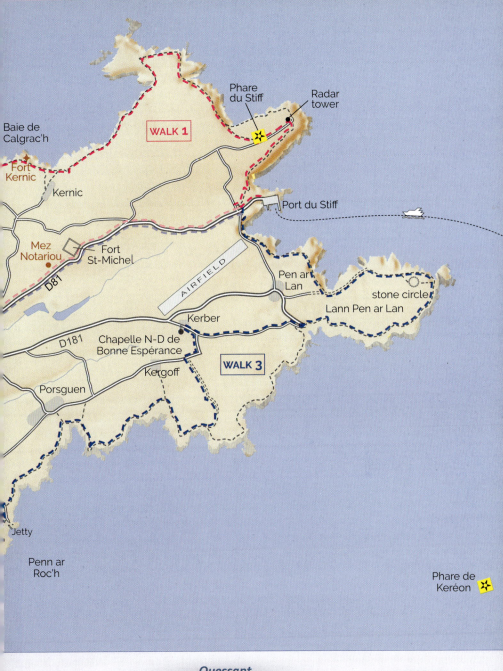

WALKING ON THE ISLAND

The three walks shown on the map are suggestions for covering nearly all the coast of the island in an organized way, or it is possible to use little roads in the interior to make up circuits. The notes offer information about points of interest on the way, but the scenery is the real highlight. The north coast from the Port du Stiff to the Pointe de Pern in the far west offers the most dramatic coastal walking. If you are only on a day trip and pressed for time, Walk 2 would offer the absolute best of the island.

Ouessant - Walk 1
Linear   Grade 1   LE STIFf to LAMPAUL via north coast   10.4km

Start from the Port du Stiff, either on arrival, or by taking the shuttle bus out from Lampaul. Walk north toward the Phare du Stiff and modern radar tower (see map on p.40/1).

Le Stiff The oldest working lighthouse in Europe was first put in place by Vauban, Louis XIV's Chief Engineer in 1695. Originally coal-powered, then with oil lamps, it began to use petrol from 1889. It is now electrified and operated automatically from the Phare du Créac'h. The building is overshadowed today by the 75m radar tower built in 1982 to monitor the *rail d'Ouessant*, a shipping channel north of the island to avoid the dangerous short-cut between Ouessant and the main land which led to many shipwrecks. The most famous of these was the Castle Drummond which went down in 1896 with the loss of 248 lives en route between Cape Town and Southampton.

Île de Keller This island with its single house is in private ownership and used as a holiday home. The oil-tanker *Olympic Bravery* which shed its load offshore here in 1976 ended up in the channel Penn ar Ru Meur, which separates the Île de Keller from the shore. A legend says the island is haunted by a 'Red Devil', man or part man part horse, whose appearance portends a storm.

Fort de Kernic This now ruined fort was built in 1862 on the same model as its partner, the Fort de Locqueltas (see p.143).

Baie de Calgrac'h At low tide, remains of the Greek *Mykonos* which was wrecked in 1936 can still be seen. Among the cargo were white Merinos sheep, some of which were very much alive and breeding on the island afterwards!

Fort de Kernic

Ouessant - Walk 2
Circular Grade 1 LAMPAUL to POINTE de PERN 8.25km

Start from the *bourg* of Lampaul. Walk in the direction of the Pointe de Pern, following the northern shore of the Bay of Lampaul (see map on p.140/1).

Loqueltas The name of the hamlet (= Loc Gueltas) means holy place of Gueltas, the Breton name of St Gildas, another evangelizing British saint said to have come to root out paganism on the island perhaps in the 6th century. The Chapelle de Notre-Dame de Bon Voyage (late 19*th* century) and *fontaine* is on the site of an older foundation, which may have been associated with St Gildas.

Fort de Locqueltas This was built as a general surveillance point in 1861, part of Napoléon III's plans which have left almost identical forts dotted around the coast of Brittany. There is another on the north coast of Ouessant. Troops were stationed here briefly at the end of the 19th century.

Pointe de Pern According to a late 18th century account, the remains of a large pagan temple once existed here. More prosaically, the ruined building now left on this most dramatic of headlands, used to house a fog-horn, powered by horses when it was constructed in 1866. Today the name Maison des Tempêtes has stuck - it derives from a 1910 novel *Das Meer* (The Sea) about Ouessant by Bernhard Kellermann.

Phare du Nividic from Pointe de Pern

The **Phare du Nividic** (started in 1911 and completed more than twenty years later) is visible off-shore, as well as the two pylons that once carried electricity cable to this unmanned structure. Workmen involved in maintenance had to be winched across in a cradle suspended above the water.

Phare de Creac'h This distinctive black and white lighthouse from 1863, 55m high, is visitable at certain times, and houses the Museé des Phares et Balises in its former electricity station. This exhibition looks at the history and mechanics of marine signalling. There is also information here about the archaeological digs at Mez Notariou (see p.146).

Moulin de Karaes This little windmill (recently restored) is the only survivor of more than forty that were used to grind grain (mostly barley) after WWII.

Eco-musée du Niou This enclave of two houses and outbuildings preserves evidence of former life on Ouessant and works to keep traditions alive. Here you can see typical furniture, clothes and tools, as well as the famous black Ouessant sheep, ironically rather scarce on the island now (see Calgrac'h).

Ouessant - Walk 3
Linear Grade 1 LE STIFf to LAMPAUL via south coast 16.8km

Start: Either take the shuttle bus and start from the **Port du Stiff** or walk out along the coast from **Lampaul** and take the bus back at the end (check times beforehand), or return on foot via the D181 (see map on p.141).

From the port, go up the road from the harbour and turn left onto the coastal path after a lavoir. Some of the cliff edges in the first section are inaccessible and fragile, so please respect signage.

Penn ar Lan The reason often given for St Pol's arrival (see opposite) was a determination to drive out pagan practices well-established on the island. There was said to be a centre of witches around the area of the Neolithic stone circle (c2000BC) here at Penn ar Lan. The saint drove them away, and the little white cross (1704, the oldest on the island) and boulder supposedly displaying the imprint of his knees after much prayer commemorate this. But the witches only went to the other extreme at the Pointe de Pern (see page 143).

Kerber and Chapelle Notre-Dame de Bonne Esperance This little chapel (rebuilt in 1854) in the hamlet of Kerber has some unremarkable statues, and modern stained glass windows by well-known artist, Pierre Toulhoat. Houses in the vicinity were built with stones from a manor house that once stood near the chapel. This was owned by the Marquis de Rieux who bought the island in 1589.

Feunteun Vélen It is easy to cut out this peninsula and return to the *bourg* via Porsguen or Toulalan if time is pressing, but it's a pleasant walk out past the **Pyramide du Runiou,** a white daymark for shipping, above the Pointe de Roc'h Hir, with views toward Molène and the Phare du Jument. The jetty at Penn ar Roc'h is where local heroine Rose Héré managed to bring in sailors from a lifeboat from the shipwrecked *Vesper* which struck rocks at the Pointe de Pern in 1903. (The spilt cargo of barrels of wine was also 'rescued' by the locals.)

Legend makes **Porz Doun** where St Guenolé lived during his dispute with St Gildas across the Baie de Lampaul. The great rock in the bay, **Youc'h Korz**, is the result of a throwing match between the two holy men. In 1924 the mail boat went down near this rock and women washing clothes on the shore at **Porz Koret** were surprised to see a cow which had been on board emerge on the beach before them.

Above the **Plage du Prat** are a spring, in legend created by St Guenolé striking the ground with his staff, and a *lavoir* in a pretty setting. Along the coast here around **Nérodin**, 'red' and other seaweeds are collected by the company Algues et Mer and processed for use in the cosmetics, health and food industries.

Lampaul

Lampaul
The *bourg* contains all the island commercial outlets and hotels, and the tourist office. The name means 'sacred place of St Pol' and it is here that the Welsh saint (one of the seven Founding Saints of Brittany, with his cathedral in St-Pol-de-Léon) is said to have arrived in about 517, to evangelize the island. The Église de St-Pol-Aurelien here was rebuilt in the 1860s on the site of earlier religious foundations. Its bell-tower was only completed in 1897 thanks to English donations in gratitude for islanders' attempts to save the lives of those shipwrecked on the Castle Drummond (see p.142).

The village port of Porspaul is sometimes used by the ferry in times of bad weather. Just above the harbour here stands the cross of St-Nicolas, on the spot where a chapel to the saint, patron of sailors, once stood.

Archaeology At Mez Notariou, on-going archaeological digs since 1988 have unearthed a late Bronze Age/early Iron Age village site, showing early settled habitation of the island, with many finds indicating the island's international links at that early period. It was also a well-established cult centre: signs of sudden destruction in the early 6th century AD may relate to tales of St Pol's mission to destroy paganism on the island. A display about the site can be seen at the Musée des Phares et Balises.

Fort St-Michel In 1898 this huge fort (well-barricaded today) was built in the interior of the island at a time of political tension between French and British colonial intentions in Africa, when defence of the French coast was potentially important. The arrival of ill-disciplined colonial troops destabilized the traditional island population, and with many men away at sea, women were especially vulnerable. André Savignon's novel *Filles de la pluie* (1912) examined these very difficult times and won the Prix Goncourt. The whole issue is little talked about today.

Lighthouses Because of the dangerous waters surrounding the island, Ouessant is ringed by lighthouses. Arrival from Molène across the Fromeur, a strait of very powerful currents, is past the Phare de Keréon (completed 1916). Off the south-west tip of the island is the Phare de la Jument (completed 1911), and in the tumultuous seas off the Pointe de Pern, the Phare de Nividic (begun in 1911 and finished in 1934). There are two land-based lighthouses on the island. Le Stiff and the Phare du Créac'h (see Walks 1 and 2). The latter houses the Musée des Phares et Balises, which explains the signalling systems.

Proëlla This special funerary rite was developed because of the frequent loss at sea and hence un-recovered bodies of islanders, often in the service of the French navy. It became customary for the priest to perform a service for such victims, including a night of vigil at their family house, using a tiny wax cross to represent the deceased. These crosses were blessed by a bishop before being placed in the special little mausoleum in the churchyard. (Note that it is aligned north-south, unlike the usual east-west orientation for graves.) Whilst awaiting a bishop's visit, the crosses would be placed in the large urn decorated with tear-drops (that look a bit like tadpoles) attached to one of the pillars in the choir inside the church.

Urn

INDEX OF PLACES

Aulne, river	53,54,104,126,130, 135,137	La Feuillée	45,120,124
		Lac de Guerlédan	126
		Lac St-Michel	118,124
Barnenez	68	Lampaul (Ouessant)	138,139,142,143,144,145
Beuzec	110,113		
Black mountains	54	Lampaul-Guimiliau	41
Brest	14-21,87,126,138	Landévennec	85,104-6
		Lannéguy	64
Cap de la Chèvre	107-9,110	Le Cloître St-Thégonnec	47,115
Cap Sizun	103,113	Le Conquet	81,100,138
Carhaix	22-7,134	Locquirec	72,74
Château de Dinan	70,107	Locronan	
Châteauneuf-du-Faou	130,132	Loqueffret	115
Crozon peninsula	25,54,55,100,103.107,110	Lostmarc'h	107
		Meneham	70,98-9
Doëlan	71,96-7	Menez Dregan	88.90
Douarnenez, Bay of	55,110	Menez Hom	53,54,55,58,85,114.135
Dourduff-en-Mer	76-8	Menez Meur	125
		Menhir de Kerloas	36,37
Flèche, river	38	Mont St-Michel-de-Brasparts	114,115,118,119,121
Gouézec	52-4	Montagnes noires	54,59
Gwaker	130	Monts d'Arrée	7,45,54,59,114-22
		Mougau Bihan	115,122,124
Huelgoat	48-51		
Hyères, river	22,24,126	Nantes	134
		Nantes-Brest Canal	7,54,126-37
Isole, river	59,61		
		Ouessant	7,100,138-46
Kastel Koz	110,112		
Keriégu	133	Penmarc'h	71,88,92-95
Kerity	93	Penn Enez	79

Plougastel		Scaër	59	
Plougonvelin	100,103	St-Derrien	38	
Plouguerneau	79,81	St-Guenolé	95	
Pointe de Doubidy	71,85-7	St-Michel	79,81	
Pointe de la Torche	92	St-Rivoal	115,125	
Pointe du Millier	110-13			
Pointe du Raz	70,113	Trémazan	82,83	
Pointe du Van	103,113	Trépassés, Baie des	113	
Pointe St-Mathieu	76,100,102	Tuchenn Gador	114,118,121,124	
Pont Coblant	54,134,135	Ty Men	133,134	
Pont Daoulas (Carhaix)	128			
Pont de Goariva	126,128	Yeun Elez	115,118,121	
Pont L'Abbé	88,95			
Pors Lanvers	112,113			
Pors Péron	112			
Pors Poulhan	88,91			
Porz Koubou	107			
Pouldavid	57			

Queffleuth, river	44,45,46
Quélarn	66,67,68
Quimper	28-35,61,63,67,106,137

Rade de Brest	14,16,21,36,71,85, 87,100,104,126,137
Riec-sur-Belon	64-5
Roc'h Ruz	114,119,121
Roc'h Trédudon	45,121
Roc'h Trévézel	114
Roches du Diable	62-3
Roscoff	11-13,114
Rosvéguen	126,133,134

GLOSSARY

allée couverte	covered passage grave
blé noir	buckwheat/sarrasin
bourg	village centre
calvaire	calvary
coiffe	lace headdress
dolmen	Neolithic burial chamber
éperon barré	fortified peninsula
fontaine	spring
grève	beach
halage / contra halage	towpath / path on opposite side of canal
landes	moor
lavoir	outdoor washing-pool
mairie	town hall
menhir	Neolithic standing-stone
moulin	mill
nemeton	Celtic sacred space/grove
passerelle	footbridge
phare	lighthouse
pilhaouer/chiffonier	rag-and-bone man
quévaise	medieval land tenure
rade	roadstead
rochers	rock formations
tourbières	peat bogs/marshes
viviers	fish-pools

Other books by Wendy Mewes

Red Dog Books
Things to see and do at the end of the World: a guide to Finistère
Walking and other activities in Finistère
The Nantes-Brest Canal: a guide
Crossing Brittany (travelogue)
Discovering the History of Brittany
Walking the Brittany Coast: Vol.2 Morlaix to Benodet
Legends of Brittany
The Saints' Shore Way
The Shape of Mist (short stories in English and French)

Footprint Guides
Brittany
Brittany West Coast

Signal Books
Brittany : a cultural history (Landscapes of the Imagination series)

Wendy Mewes is a writer who lives in Finistère. She is the author of many books and articles about Brittany, and works extensively in promoting Breton history and culture to English-speaking visitors through talks, courses and guided visits. History, landscape and walking are her areas of special interest.

Website
www.wendymewes.com
Blog
www.wendymewes.blogspot.com

Other titles published by Red Dog Books

by G H Randall
  Brittany's Green Ways
  Walks in Côtes d'Armor

by Judy Smith
  Walking Brittany
  Walking the Brittany Coast: Vol 1 Mont St-Michel to Morlaix

by Wendy Mewes
  Things to see and do in Huelgoat
  Things to see and do in the Monts d'Arrée

For full details see the Red Dog Books website
www.reddogbooks.com